Investing, Collecting & Trading in
Certified Commemoratives

An in-depth analysis of gold & silver issues: 1892 – 1954

By:
Harry Laibstain

Investing, Collecting & Trading In Certified Commemoratives

Copyright © 1995 by Harry Laibstain

ALL RIGHTS RESERVED. No part of this book may be reproduced or utilized, by any means, without permission in writing from the publisher, except by a reviewer who wishes to quote brief excerpts in connection with a review in a newspaper or magazine.

ISBN 1-880731-24-X perfect binding • 1-880731-51-7 spiral binding
1-880731-50-9 hardcover

Library of Congress Catalog Number 94-80033

DLRC Press
6095 Indian River Road, Suite #204
Virginia Beach, Virginia 23464
(804) 424-0560 • fax (804) 424-2363

Printed in the United States of America

Dedicated to my parents
Sarah & Nathan —
I can never thank them enough —

and to my family
Sherry, Mandy & Katie
who give my life
meaning and make
it all worthwhile.

Acknowledgments

Photos in this book were taken by Tom Mulvaney unless otherwise stated.

I would like to thank the following for permission to reprint information from their publications: Professional Coin Grading Service-Population Report; NGC-*Census Report*; CDN, Inc.-*The Coin Dealer Newsletter* and *The Certified Coin Dealer Newsletter*; Western Publishing Company-"A Guidebook of United States Coins" by R.S. Yeoman.

Dave and John Feigenbaum for the encouragement to write this book.

Cindy Ames for her incredible stamina in typing and retyping this manuscript and for managing to read my handwritten rough drafts.

Dennis Baker, editor of *CDN* and *CCDN*, for his intelligent discussion of the issues as they relate to pricing. Even if he didn't always agree with me.

My wife, Sherry, and children, Mandy and Katie, who gave me the time and positive feedback necessary to complete this project.

Lynn Feigenbaum, Public Editor of *The Virginian-Pilot and the Ledger-Star*, for editing this book.

A special thanks to contributors: Larry Shepherd, a long-time friend and fellow dealer, for writing the foreword. Yitzy Gedalowitz, another long-time friend and colleague, for writing a highly knowledgeable chapter on his specialty, proof-like commems.

Thanks to my hardworking staff – John Noonan, Joy Wigglesworth and Cindy Ames – for covering the office while I worked on this book and for giving me general assistance and input throughout.

Foreword

by Larry Shepherd

When I first started collecting coins, commemoratives were not widely collected and there was very little information available about them other than the brief descriptions and mintage figures found in the *Red Book*. Since the 1970's however, much has changed. Commems (as they are called within the hobby) are now one of the most popularly collected and widely written about series in current numismatics.

This surge in popularity is not hard to understand. Numerous books and expanded coverage in numismatic publications helped to introduce scores of collectors to the beauty and the collectibility of commemoratives. Many collectors came to realize, as I did, that no other series of U.S. coins combines as much artistic diversity, historical background, low mintages, and yet, accessibility as commems. Despite the fact that 70 of the 144 different dates in the series have a mintage under 10,000 pieces, nearly all are within the price range of a vast number of collectors. The popularity of commems has been further enhanced by the realization that many commems can be found with striking eye appeal, their artistic beauty accented by rich rolling luster or toning in a broad spectrum of colors.

The growth in popularity of commems has fueled a quest for knowledge and information in recent years. Several outstanding books and published articles have added to collectors' understanding of the historical background, minting, and sale of the 50 different issues, but little has been written to help the collector or investor make informed decisions in the marketplace. *Investing, Collecting & Trading in Certified Commemoratives* by Harry Laibstain fills that void. Whether you are an experienced commem collector or are a beginner, you will find much in this book that can help you.

Most of the information in the following chapters is not discernable from mintage figures or price sheets. Harry uses population tables of certified commems and his own extensive experience in the marketplace to shed new light on the subjects of scarcity, popularity and value. If you want to know why a high mintage Sesquicentennial half dollar is worth more in MS65 condition than the extremely low mintage 1935/34-D or S Boone, this book will tell you. If you are wondering whether a particular issue is scarce or whether it is common with good luster or a strong strike, chances are you will find the answer here. And if you are unsure of the remarketability of a particular coin in a certain grade and holder that you are thinking of buying, here's the place to check – before you write the check!

I have known Harry Laibstain for several years as mutual customers, as a knowledgeable and trustworthy competitor and as a good friend. It would be hard to find anyone more qualified to write a book on commemoratives with such a wealth of market information. Harry is an experienced veteran of the bourse floors and one of the most active market makers of commemoratives in the popular collector grades, mint state 63 through 66. It would be safe to bet that he buys and sells more commems in these grades in a typical month than most dealers (or authors) would handle in a year.

Collecting commemoratives can be fun, it can be interesting, and if done right, it can be profitable. Regardless of whether your objective is to buy for outright enjoyment or to sell at a profit, or both, this book can help you. Thank you, Harry, for sharing your experience with the countless collectors and investors who will benefit from this book.

Larry Shepherd
SIMCO Numismatics
January 1995

Introduction

A great deal of credit for getting me to write this book must go to Dave Feigenbaum and his son, John, who are my publishers. I met Dave in 1980 at a small coin show in Hampton, Virginia. I still recall the purchase I made from Dave that day. The coins were unimportant but Dave's salesmanship and enthusiasm stuck with me. We continued to have contact at local shows but did not become close until 1985, when we began to travel the national show circuit together. Several years later John began to accompany his father on our trips and we also became good friends.

I have been considering this book since 1990. It was during that time that Dave and John first approached me about a book on commemoratives. Dave's success as an author and their growing publishing business kept the discussion going. Finally, in 1994, I decided to go ahead with the project. But, what I had once envisioned as a quick little summation of the data became an involved analysis of each issue. It took months of working at home, in the mornings and on weekends, to formulate and polish the essays into readable form. Each issue went through several rewrites. When the date-by-date analysis pages were ready to hand over I was immensely relieved. They would now move on to Dave's wife Lynn, a newspaper editor, for final editing.

Producing this work was an educational experience. One obvious benefit is that I know more about commems than I did before. In addition, I gained a better understanding and respect for communicating technical information to a wider audience. Finally, I learned that putting together a project like this takes a lot of time and work from everyone involved. It was probably a blessing that I underestimated this task; otherwise I might have become permanently sidetracked.

In the end I am happy with the outcome. Everything is here that you need to make intelligent commemorative transactions. Let this book be your adviser. It will enable you to maximize your return.

If you have any questions or information regarding this book or issues pertaining to certification, please contact me. I can be reached at:

Harry Laibstain Rare Coins
11817 Canon Boulevard, Suite #202
Newport News, VA 23606
804-873-6720 • FAX: 804-873-1977

January 1995

Table of Contents

Acknowledgements iv
Foreword *by Larry Shepherd* v
Introduction vi

Chapter 1: How To Use This Book 1
    Mintage 2
    Population 3
    Grade Rankings 3
    Pricing 3
    PDS Sets 6
    Percentage Of Mintage Which Is Certified 6
    Popular Grades and Background 7
    Evaluation 7
    Recommendations 7

Chapter 2: Introduction To Commemoratives 9
    The Market 11
    PCGS versus NGC 12
    Can Coin Prices Rebound? 12
    An Even Playing Field 13
    The Future 14

Chapter 3: The Silver Commemoratives 15

Chapter 4: The Gold Commemoratives 107

Chapter 5: Proof-Like Commemoratives
    by Yitzy Gedalowitz 121

Appendix A: Glossary 126
Appendix B: Statistics 127
Appendix C: References 134
About The Author 135

Listing Of Tables

#	Title	Page
1	Silver commems ranked by mintage with PDS sets & related issues removed	2
2	Silver commems ranked by mintage with PDS sets & related issues grouped by "type"	2
3	Ranking in MS63 with PDS & related issses removed	4
4	Ranking in MS63 with PDS & related issses grouped by "type"	4
5	Ranking in MS64 with PDS & related issses removed	4
6	Ranking in MS64 with PDS & related issses grouped by "type"	4
7	Ranking MS65 with PDS & related issses removed	5
8	Ranking in MS65 with PDS & related issses grouped by "type"	5
9	Ranking MS66 with PDS & related issses removed	5
10	Ranking MS66 with PDS & related issses grouped by "type"	5
11	NGC populations of proof-like commems	123
A-1	Rank of silver & gold commems by mintage	127
A-2	PCGS & NGC populations in MS64-67 (Dec. 1994 data)	128
A-3	Rank of silver & gold commems by total mint state population (PCGS & NGC combined)	129
A-4	Rank of silver & gold commems by % of mintage which is certified	130
A-5	Silver & gold commems ranked by MS64 population	131
A-6	Silver & gold commems ranked by MS65 population	132
A-7	Silver & gold commems ranked by MS66 population	133

Chapter 1

How To Use This Book

How To Use This Book

Welcome to the complex and interesting world of certified commemoratives. This work is different from previous books on the subject. Its purpose is to provide a better understanding of important factors that relate to each issue's scarcity and value. Little time is spent on design, production or historic context of each coin. This information has been well documented by other authors.

I have divided this book into four major sections plus an appendix. There is also a chapter on proof-like issues by Yitzy Gedalozwitz, an expert on the subject. Chapter 1 explains how to use the date-by-date analysis pages. In addition, it documents the sources and explains the rationale for the information presented. The second chapter is an introduction to commemoratives and the marketplace, with basics about collecting. More importantly, Chapter 2 contains background information about the certified market that should prove invaluable to serious commemorative enthusiasts.

Chapters 3 and 4 are an in-depth analysis of all silver and gold commemoratives, both single issues and PDS sets. Each mintmark receives its own statistics and evaluation. All issues are detailed by mintage, population, grade ranking and values. Individual commentary and tips are included with important ratios, selected grades and a short background on each issue.

Mintage

Mintage figures were taken from the 1994 *Redbook*. The rankings discussed represent each coin's relationship to the 144 pieces in the silver set and the 13 pieces in the gold set (modern commemoratives are excluded). All coins have been ranked individually.

The tables to the right provide two other perspectives regarding mintage rankings. *Table 1* lists everything but the PDS issues or coins from their series. Individual two-coin issues have been left in. *Table 2* treats all issues as type coins by combining multi-year and mintmarked issues.

As you see, rankings are dramatically affected when viewed in different ways. With PDS issues

Table 1: Silver commems ranked by mintage with PDS sets & related issues removed

RANK	DATE/TYPE	MINTAGE
1	Grant/Star	4,256
2	Miss. 2X4	5,000
3	Ala. 2X2	6,006
4	Hawaiian	9,958
5	Hudson	10,008
6	Sp. Trail	10,008
7	Vancouver	14,994
8	New Rochelle	15,266
9	Missouri	15,428
10	Norfolk	16,936
11	Albany	17,671
12	Antietam	18,028
13	Lynchburg	20,013
14	Elgin	20,015
15	1921 Pilgrim	20,053
16	Delaware	20,993
17	Isabella	24,214
18	Bridgeport	25,015
19	Maryland	25,015
20	Wisconsin	25,015
21	York	25,015
22	Conn.	25,018
23	Robinson	25,265
24	Gettys.	26,928
25	Pan-Pac	27,134
26	Vermont	28,142
27	Roanoke	29,030
28	'36-D San Diego	30,092
29	Lafayette	36,026
30	Maine	50,028
31	Cleveland	50,030
32	Alabama	59,038
33	Grant	67,405
34	'35-S San Deigo	70,132
35	Bay Bridge	71,424
36	Long Is.	81,826
37	Calif.	86,594
38	Lexington	100,057
39	Iowa	100,058
40	Sesqui	141,120
41	Hugenot	142,080
42	1920 Pilgrim	152,112
43	Lincoln	162,013
44	Monroe	274,077
45	1892 Columbian	950,000
46	Stone Mtn.	1,314,709
47	1893 Columbian	1,550,405

Table 2: Silver commems ranked by mintage with PDS sets & related issues grouped by "type"

RANK	DATE/TYPE	MINTAGE
1	Hawaiian	9,958
2	Hudson	10,008
3	Sp. Trail	10,008
4	Vancouver	14,994
5	Cinci (ALL)	15,016
6	New Rochelle	15,266
7	Norfolk	16,936
8	Albany	17,671
9	Antietam	18,028
10	Lynchburg	20,013
11	Elgin	20,015
12	Missouri (BOTH)	20,428
13	Delaware	20,993
14	Isabella	24,214
15	Bridgeport	25,015
16	Maryland	25,015
17	Wisconsin	25,015
18	York	25,015
19	Conn.	25,018
20	Columbia (ALL)	25,023
21	Robinson	25,265
22	Gettys.	26,928
23	Pan-Pac	27,134
24	Vermont	28,142
25	Roanoke	29,030
26	Lafayette	36,026
27	Maine	50,028
28	Cleveland	50,030
29	Rh.Isl (ALL)	50,034
30	Alabama (BOTH)	65,044
31	Bay Bridge	71,424
32	Grant (BOTH)	71,661
33	Long Is.	81,826
34	Ark (ALL)	85,301
35	Calif.	86,594
36	Boone (ALL)	87,187
37	Lexington	100,057
38	Iowa	100,058
39	San Diego (BOTH)	100,224
40	Sesqui	141,120
41	Hugenot	142,080
42	Texas (ALL)	149,661
43	Lincoln	162,013
44	Pilgrim (BOTH)	172,165
45	Oregon (ALL)	203,102
46	Monroe	274,077
47	Stone Mtn.	1,314,709
48	W/C (ALL)	2,422,392
49	Columbian (BOTH)	2,500,405
50	BTW (ALL)	3,091,205

removed, the scarce two-coin issues line up at the top with the better single issues falling close behind. When issues are combined as type only, there is a complete turnabout compared to individual rankings of the entire set (see also *Appendix Table A-1*). Viewing commemoratives in this way leaves only one multi-year issue among the first 20%, with the majority in the bottom third. This comparison more accurately reflects the way the market ranks them (as demonstrated by price relationships).

Population

Population data were compiled using the March 1994 issue of the *PCGS Population Report* and *NGC Census*. These are available from the grading services or through your dealer for a nominal charge. I highly recommend purchasing them. Populations listed in the grids are the sum of both services' reports.

Coins are sometimes broken out of the certified holders and resubmitted. In order to keep populations accurate, PCGS pays 50 cents for the grading label inside each slab and then adjusts its records accordingly. NGC does not have a formal program but will make adjustments if information regarding regrades is furnished. Many dealers do return PCGS labels from "crack outs" although an unknown percentage are lost or kept. Because there is no refund, a smaller percentage of NGC labels are returned. Even with adjustments, combined population data are probably overstated by as much as 25% on some issues.

Coins most likely to have inflated populations are those with higher values and large price spreads between grades. The possibility of a higher grade provides the strongest incentive to crack out and resubmit coins.

At present, some PCGS coins tend to be worth more in the market than NGC coins and the latter are sometimes cracked out or submitted as "cross overs" to PCGS to gain that extra value. Additionally, lower-grade and lower-value coins are taken out of holders to go into raw sets. Since populations do not influence values at lower grade levels, inflated data here are not significant.

Grade Rankings

Populations were tallied by certified grade to create rankings. Silver issues are ranked from 1 to 144 and gold issues from 1 to 13. Grades analyzed were MS60, 62, 63, 64, 65, 66 and 67. All multi-year and PDS-set coins were considered individually. You will notice that multiple-issue coins appear scarcer than single issues, which often price dramatically higher. Many of the multiple issues have low mintages and populations. Coupled with their low prices they are somewhat underrated. However, their values are not as ridiculously low as they appear when you consider overall market demand. *Tables 3-10* rank commems by certified populations in grades 63 to 66 — first without PDS issues and then with type issues grouped. (Also see Appendix *Tables A5-A7* for comparison.)

Value of single-design coins like Barber quarters or Walking Liberty halves can be evaluated rather accurately by supply only. Since this is the traditional method of evaluation, we have followed the same format in our date-by-date analysis sections (Chapters 3 and 4). However, in a series with scores of designs, numerous subsets and varying degrees of interest (per issue), demand plays a larger role in determining availability and value. Looking at commemoratives as the market sees them allows us to inject demand into the economic equation. In order to eliminate the supply-side bias against the multi-coin issues, refer back to these tables when evaluating one- and two-coin issues.

Pricing

Prices were compiled from six different time frames. The 1957 prices come from the 10th edition of the *Redbook* and are listed in the MS63 column. The 1970 prices come from the Jan. 9 issue of the *Graysheet* and are also listed as MS63. At the time these prices were reported they simply represented uncirculated examples. For the sake of comparison I have assumed them to be this middle grade.

The next date, 1980, was chosen to represent a peak in the market. The Jan. 4 *Graysheet* was used for MS60 and MS65 prices. MS63 prices have been estimated to increase the fields of comparison. A combination of market knowledge and the relation-

Table 3: Rank of certified commems in MS63 with PDS & related issues removed

RANK	DATE/TYPE	63 POP
1	Norfolk	153
2	Sp. Trail	236
3	New Rochelle	259
4	Wisconsin	299
5	'36-D San Diego	314
6	Grant/Star	322
7	Antietam	327
8	York	352
9	Roanoke	363
10	Miss. 2X4	423
11	1921 Pilgrim	423
12	Ala. 2X2	433
13	Lafayette	449
14	Hawaiian	466
15	Missouri	470
16	Lynchburg	478
17	Alabama	484
18	Elgin	489
19	Iowa	514
20	Albany	524
21	Delaware	536
22	Vancouver	562
23	Pan-Pac	609
24	Bridgeport	623
25	Hudson	647
26	Gettys.	660
27	Maine	663
28	'35-S San Deigo	677
29	Bay Bridge	679
30	Maryland	732
31	Conn.	751
32	Hugenot	778
33	Robinson	812
34	Vermont	898
35	Isabella	919
36	Calif.	997
37	Grant	1,017
38	Monroe	1,086
39	Lexington	1,118
40	Lincoln	1,200
41	Long Is.	1,220
42	1920 Pilgrim	1,233
43	Sesqui	1,355
44	Cleveland	1,356
45	1893 Columbian	1,772
46	1892 Columbian	1,831
47	Stone Mtn.	1,894

Table 4: Rank of certified commems in MS63 with PDS & related issues grouped by "type"

RANK	DATE/TYPE	63 POP
1	Norfolk	153
2	Sp. Trail	236
3	New Rochelle	259
4	Wisconsin	299
5	Antietam	327
6	York	352
7	Roanoke	363
8	Columbia (ALL)	430
9	Lafayette	449
10	Hawaiian	466
11	Lynchburg	478
12	Elgin	489
13	Iowa	514
14	Albany	524
15	Delaware	536
16	Vancouver	562
17	Pan-Pac	609
18	Bridgeport	623
19	Hudson	647
20	Gettys.	660
21	Maine	663
22	Bay Bridge	679
23	Cinci. (ALL)	701
24	Maryland	732
25	Conn.	751
26	Hugenot	778
27	Robinson	812
28	BTW (ALL)	814
29	Missouri (ALL)	893
30	Vermont	898
31	Alabama (ALL)	917
32	Isabella	919
33	San Diego (ALL)	991
34	Calif.	997
35	Monroe	1,086
36	Rh. Island (ALL)	1,109
37	Lexington	1,118
38	W/C (ALL)	1,134
39	Lincoln	1,200
40	Long Is.	1,220
41	Grant (ALL)	1,339
42	Sesqui	1,355
43	Cleveland	1,356
44	Texas (ALL)	1,613
45	Pilgrim (ALL)	1,656
46	Stone Mtn.	1,894
47	Boone (ALL)	1,991
48	Oregon (ALL)	2,365
49	Arkansas (ALL)	2,838
50	Columbian (ALL)	3,603

Table 5: Rank of certified commems in MS64 with PDS & related issues removed

RANK	DATE/TYPE	64 POP
1	Grant/Star	296
2	Lafayette	415
3	Miss. 2X4	525
4	Norfolk	526
5	Ala. 2X2	584
6	Missouri	614
7	Hawaiian	623
8	Alabama	694
9	Pan-Pac	717
10	Sp. Trail	831
11	Isabella	889
12	Vancouver	907
13	1921 Pilgrim	927
14	Hudson	932
15	Sesqui	962
16	Monroe	999
17	Antietam	1,035
18	York	1,084
19	Maine	1,124
20	Calif.	1,162
21	Grant	1,180
22	New Rochelle	1,192
23	Vermont	1,222
24	Wisconsin	1,232
25	Lynchburg	1,241
26	Delaware	1,402
27	Conn.	1,427
28	Robinson	1,461
29	Bay Bridge	1,471
30	1893 Columbian	1,522
31	Roanoke	1,523
32	Albany	1,533
33	Lexington	1,540
34	Hugenot	1,545
35	Gettys.	1,633
36	Lincoln	1,698
37	1920 Pilgrim	1,712
38	1892 Columbian	1,761
39	Bridgeport	1,794
40	Elgin	1,806
41	Iowa	1,836
42	Long Is.	1,855
43	Maryland	1,882
44	'36-D San Diego	2,035
45	Cleveland	2,574
46	'35-S San Deigo	2,853
47	Stone Mtn.	3,118

Table 6: Rank of certified commems in MS64 with PDS & related issues grouped by "type"

RANK	DATE/TYPE	64 POP
1	Lafayette	415
2	Norfolk	526
3	Hawaiian	623
4	Pan-Pac	717
5	Sp. Trail	831
6	Isabella	889
7	Vancouver	907
8	Hudson	932
9	Sesqui	962
10	Monroe	999
11	Antietam	1,035
12	York	1,084
13	Maine	1,124
14	Missouri (ALL)	1,139
15	Calif.	1,162
16	New Rochelle	1,192
17	Vermont	1,222
18	Wisconsin	1,232
19	Lynchburg	1,241
20	Alabama (ALL)	1,278
21	Delaware	1,402
22	Conn.	1,427
23	Columbia (ALL)	1,437
24	Robinson	1,461
25	Bay Bridge	1,471
26	Grant (ALL)	1,476
27	Roanoke	1,523
28	Albany	1,533
29	Lexington	1,540
30	Hugenot	1,545
31	Gettys.	1,633
32	Cinci. (ALL)	1,639
33	Lincoln	1,698
34	Bridgeport	1,794
35	Elgin	1,806
36	Iowa	1,836
37	Long Is.	1,855
38	Maryland	1,882
39	Cleveland	2,574
40	Pilgrim (ALL)	2,639
41	Rh. Island (ALL)	3,000
42	Stone Mtn.	3,118
43	Columbian (ALL)	3,283
44	San Diego (ALL)	4,888
45	Arkansas (ALL)	5,435
46	Boone (ALL)	5,485
47	Texas (ALL)	5,634
48	W/C (ALL)	6,010
49	BTW (ALL)	6,841
50	Oregon (ALL)	7,236

Table 7: **Rank of certified commems in MS65 with PDS & related issues removed**

RANK	DATE/TYPE	65 POP
1	Grant/Star	90
2	Miss. 2X4	100
3	Sesqui	121
4	Missouri	127
5	Alabama	149
6	Lafayette	152
7	Ala. 2X2	176
8	Monroe	196
9	Hawaiian	203
10	Isabella	337
11	Pan-Pac	350
12	1893 Columbian	396
13	Hudson	434
14	1921 Pilgrim	451
15	Lexington	477
16	Vancouver	535
17	Grant	546
18	1892 Columbian	604
19	Vermont	621
20	Calif.	661
21	Maine	676
22	Hugenot	683
23	1920 Pilgrim	696
24	Robinson	749
25	Lincoln	773
26	Long Is.	878
27	Sp. Trail	940
28	Conn.	1,007
29	Maryland	1,066
30	Delaware	1,072
31	Gettys.	1,077
32	Lynchburg	1,104
33	Bridgeport	1,169
34	Norfolk	1,237
35	Bay Bridge	1,314
36	Albany	1,336
37	New Rochelle	1,340
38	Cleveland	1,365
39	Antietam	1,387
40	Stone Mtn.	1,578
41	Elgin	1,734
42	York	1,898
43	Roanoke	1,998
44	Wisconsin	2,129
45	Iowa	3,335
46	'36-D San Diego	3,835
47	'35-S San Diego	5,614

Table 8: **Rank of certified commems in MS65 with PDS & related issues grouped by "type"**

RANK	DATE/TYPE	65 POP
1	Sesqui	121
2	Lafayette	152
3	Monroe	196
4	Hawaiian	203
5	Missouri (ALL)	227
6	Alabama (ALL)	325
7	Isabella	337
8	Pan-Pac	350
9	Hudson	434
10	Lexington	477
11	Vancouver	535
12	Vermont	621
13	Grant (ALL)	636
14	Calif.	661
15	Maine	676
16	Hugenot	683
17	Robinson	749
18	Lincoln	773
19	Cinci. (ALL)	849
20	Long Is.	878
21	Sp. Trail	940
22	Columbian (ALL)	1,000
23	Conn.	1,007
24	Maryland	1,066
25	Delaware	1,072
26	Gettys.	1,077
27	Lynchburg	1,104
28	Pilgrim (ALL)	1,147
29	Bridgeport	1,169
30	Norfolk	1,237
31	Bay Bridge	1,314
32	Albany	1,336
33	New Rochelle	1,340
34	Cleveland	1,365
35	Antietam	1,387
36	Stone Mtn.	1,578
37	Elgin	1,734
38	York	1,898
39	Roanoke	1,998
40	Wisconsin	2,129
41	Columbia (ALL)	2,141
42	Rh. Island (ALL)	2,177
43	Arkansas (ALL)	3,011
44	W/C (ALL)	3,235
45	Iowa	3,335
46	Boone (ALL)	5,832
47	BTW (ALL)	8,232
48	Oregon (ALL)	8,552
49	Texas (ALL)	9,093
50	San Diego (ALL)	9,449

Table 9: **Rank of certified commems in MS66 with PDS & related issues removed**

RANK	DATE/TYPE	66 POP
1	Miss. 2X4	3
2	Alabama	5
3	Sesqui	5
4	Missouri	8
5	Ala. 2X2	12
6	Grant/Star	14
7	Lafayette	20
8	Hawaiian	25
9	Monroe	38
10	1893 Columbian	42
11	Lexington	54
12	1921 Pilgrim	55
13	Hudson	68
14	1892 Columbian	81
15	Grant	89
16	1920 Pilgrim	115
17	Isabella	116
18	Vancouver	128
19	Vermont	129
20	Pan-Pac	133
21	Hugenot	142
22	Long Is.	158
23	Lincoln	168
24	Maine	175
25	Robinson	200
26	Bridgeport	214
27	Conn.	222
28	Maryland	224
29	Gettys.	231
30	Cleveland	252
31	Calif.	269
32	Sp. Trail	285
33	Delaware	295
34	'36-D San Diego	334
35	Stone Mtn.	349
36	Lynchburg	361
37	New Rochelle	363
38	Albany	419
39	Bay Bridge	420
40	Elgin	461
41	Antietam	538
42	Roanoke	717
43	'35-S San Diego	831
44	Wisconsin	991
45	York	1,158
46	Norfolk	1,415
47	Iowa	1,782

Table 10: **Rank of certified commems in MS66 with PDS & related issues grouped by "type"**

RANK	DATE/TYPE	66 POP
1	Sesqui	5
2	Missouri (ALL)	11
3	Alabama (ALL)	17
4	Lafayette	20
5	Hawaiian	25
6	Monroe	38
7	Lexington	54
8	Hudson	68
9	Grant (ALL)	103
10	Isabella	116
11	Columbian (ALL)	123
12	Vancouver	128
13	Vermont	129
14	Pan-Pac	133
15	Hugenot	142
16	Cinci. (ALL)	151
17	Long Is.	158
18	Lincoln	168
19	Pilgrim (ALL)	170
20	Maine	175
21	Robinson	200
22	Bridgeport	214
23	Conn.	222
24	Maryland	224
25	Gettys.	231
26	Cleveland	252
27	Calif.	269
28	W/C (ALL)	275
29	Sp. Trail	285
30	Delaware	295
31	Stone Mtn.	349
32	Lynchburg	361
33	New Rochelle	363
34	Albany	419
35	Bay Bridge	420
36	Arkansas (ALL)	420
37	Rh. Island (ALL)	450
38	Elgin	461
39	Antietam	538
40	Roanoke	717
41	Wisconsin	991
42	BTW (ALL)	1,057
43	York	1,158
44	San Diego (ALL)	1,165
45	Columbia (ALL)	1,302
46	Norfolk	1,415
47	Iowa	1,782
48	Boone (ALL)	1,798
49	Texas (ALL)	4,158
50	Oregon (ALL)	4,227

ship of 1982 MS63 prices to MS60 and MS65 was used to develop these numbers. The 1982 prices represent a market low and were selected from the Oct. 1 *Graysheet*. MS60, MS63 and MS65 prices come directly from this price guide and MS66 levels are estimated. These estimates were made by assessing grade rarity and combining it with the ratios between the 1989 and 1994 MS65 and MS66 prices.

Prices from 1989 were selected as another market peak and it was here that many commemoratives reached their all-time highs. The June 2 issue of the *Gray* and *Bluesheets** were used. MS60, MS63, MS64 and MS65 prices come from the *Graysheet* and MS62, MS66 and MS67 from the *Bluesheet*. In some cases the lowest grades had to be adjusted slightly to make the difference between them realistic. For example, occasionally the *Graysheet* MS60 listing would be higher than *Bluesheet* MS62. This and other similar situations generally occurred on issues with very tight spreads. Changes were minor and of little significance.

The 1994 prices were selected as a market low since commems, like many other rare coins, spent 5 years searching for the bottom. The March 25 issues of the *Gray* and *Blue* sheets were used to represent this year. Like 1989, the *Graysheet* contributed MS60, MS63, MS64 and MS65 while the *Bluesheet* the MS62, MS66 and MS67. As before, minor price adjustments were made to some of the lower grades to adjust *Bluesheet* MS62 levels in line with those of the *Graysheet*. Some additional minor adjustments were necessary as spreads became even tighter in the down market.

PDS Sets

PDS issues have been analyzed individually to show the price relationships among coins in the same set. Only a few sets have pieces with similar rarities in every grade. In addition, the certification of coins has caused many sets to be broken up as collectors and investors purchase the specific issues they like or assemble their own sets. Today the term "set" often means more than coins with similar colorations. Many collectors also demand sets that are consistently graded. These demands are often unmet by original sets. Most importantly, dealers trade these issues as single coins on the electronic trading networks. A review of the prices posted on these exchanges demonstrates just how different each coin within the set can be.

Some sets have unequal rarity from the lowest grades. More often, related issues will start off with similar values but end up with different ones. Rarity in higher grades can fluctuate widely even in sets with similar mintages. Part of the reason the scarcer issues from PDS sets are undervalued is a result of unclear reporting. Because the *Gray* and *Bluesheets* currently lack the space to price these issues separately they are only listed as sets in these price guides.

Theoretically, prices for PDS sets are the sum of the three issues. Unfortunately, some of the same confusion that surrounds individual prices trickles down to set totals. Some 1994 prices represent sets where the sum of the parts is significantly less than the total, while in others the sum is significantly greater. These instances are denoted under the 1994 set pricing with either one asterisk (* – the set total is greater than the sum of its parts) or two (** – the set total is less than the sum of its parts). For an example, see the 1935/34 Boone. Individual 1994 pricing in the highlighted gray box is meant to show the relationship between coins within a set. These prices were developed using data from the electronic trading networks and my own experience in dealer to dealer transactions.

Percent of Mintage Which is Certified

The percent of mintage certified ranges from less than 1% to 31% for silver commems and up to 41% for gold commems. This supplies us with crucial information regarding future supply.

The buying and selling of high-grade commemoratives is dominated by certified coins. Our current situation reminds me of a race where both supply and demand are increasing at a steady pace. Some dealers argue that the supply of these commemorative coins, minted 1954 and before, is fixed and that the only variable is demand. This may be technically true but the reality is different. The bull markets

---

* All Bluesheet prices are bids for PCGS coins.

in certified coins were ignited by low populations and fueled by low supply. Essentially, if a high-grade coin is not in the holder of a recognized grading service it has very little effect on supply and prices. This is why these percentages are so important. As the flow of uncertified coins begins to dwindle, supply will slow and eventually become a tiny drip. When will that time come? No one has the answer but careful study of these percentages and how they change in the future will give us important insights.

Popular Grades and Background

This information is taken from my personal experience. Collectors tend to purchase somewhat lower grades than investors but in many cases there is some overlap. The extreme low end has been left out as most of these coins trade at basal values.

The history of our commemorative coinage is extremely colorful and educational. However, it has been well covered in other books. I have only given a brief statement here to distinguish each issue. For further reading I recommend "Commemorative Coins of the United States" by Q. David Bowers and "Silver and Gold Commemorative Coins" by Anthony Swiatek and Walter Breen.

Evaluation

The sections with comments and tips are self explanatory and designed to flesh out the numbers for the commemorative enthusiast. I have tried to highlight trends, tell how the coin comes and compare the issue to its price. The tips section was used to highlight important information already discussed or to add an additional tidbit that didn't get into the essay. Use this for a quick reference.

Recommendations

Many issues in this book are recommended and these apply to the grades listed in the author's choice section. Coins that are *highly recommended* are currently undervalued in relation to similar issues and should out-perform the overall market. Issues that receive a *recommended* status are properly but not necessarily fully priced. These issues also have good growth potential if commemoratives or the larger market for rare coins move up. They also have limited downside risk, which tends to characterize the entire commemorative market. Coins without recommendations may be overpriced or fully priced in the current market. Many times these issues suffer from an oversupply and do not have the same upside potential as the scarcer coins. However, truth is stranger than fiction. These plentiful issues are often the choice of mass marketers who are able to get large quantities of a single issue off the market (and the price rises).

The author's choice section represents the grades I feel are most appropriate for the individual commemorative buyer. Collector choices are based on a combination of affordability and value while investment choices are based on future potential and rarity as well as aforementioned factors. Individual grade recommendations may differ from your own choices. Do not get hung up on the grades I chose. In many cases, selecting a grade meant a choice between two. On another day, some coins would have been picked one grade differently. Take this as a general guideline.

Chapter 2

Introduction To Commemoratives

Introduction To Commemoratives

Now that you know how to use this book, along with some other things I managed to slip into the first chapter, let's talk about commemoratives – the market past and present, grading services, bids and a scenario for the future.

Commemorative coins are distinctly different from all other series due to the multitude of designs. In the silver issues there are 50 different coins, often referred to as the 50-piece type set. When PDS coins and other multiple issues are added, there are 144 individual dates and mintmarks. In the gold issues there are 10 different designs and a total of 13 coins.

Commemorative coins combine diversity of design with the richness of history. Every issue marks some historical event or pays tribute to someone or something significant in the annals of our country. With so many opportunities for artistic expression, commemorative coins – particularly the larger silver issues – exhibit some stunning artwork. These coins were not issued for business purposes, like Washington quarters and Walking Liberty halves, so their designers were not under the same constraints to please the public at large. Freed of this traditional censorship, commemorative issues were able to step up to a higher artistic platform and often did.

An 1893 Columbian certified MS64 by PCGS

A Vancouver certified MS65 by NGC

Another appealing aspect of commemorative issues is, and always will be, their low mintages. Collectors and investors have always gravitated towards "sexy" low mintages. Many commemorative buyers focus on these issues. Low mintage coins are likely to be hoarded and this increases their scarcity in the marketplace. Some low mintage coins, mainly those from PDS sets, can be purchased for well under $200 in nice mint-state grades. The MS64 1938 Arkansas and Oregon Trails from the same year are good examples. Compare these to any low-mintage coins from regular business issues and you will be impressed with the difference in market prices.

Commemorative issues are also unique in the many ways they can be collected. In addition to the standard methods of collecting by type or completing the set, the commemorative series offers numerous subsets. Multi-year mint-marked sets like Arkansas (15 coins), Boone (16 coins), Oregon Trail (14 coins), Texas (13 coins), Booker T. Washington (18 coins) and Washington Carver (12 coins) are all very popular and highly collected subsets of the complete series. Collectors are also likely to focus on other 3-coin PDS sets, double issues like Missouris and Alabamas or coins that have some historical relation to each other like the four Civil War commems – Antietam, Gettysburg, Lincoln and Grant. Other popular subsets are coins with ships (6 different types), eagles (7 types) and animals (10 types).

Some coins besides PDS sets were issued and distributed together. Several of these include gold and silver commemoratives, and are very popular. The most important is the Panama-Pacific Exposition set, which includes four gold issues and one silver coin. These were issued in varying forms of sets and many remain intact today (see Bowers for a complete explanation and history of Pan-Pac sets). Complete sets are expensive due to the inclusion of the two $50 pieces. The three more affordable coins – the half dollar, the dollar and the $2.50 – are often collected together. The Grant four-coin set includes two gold and two silver issues, each offering a no-star and with-star variety. Finally there is the Sesquicentennial $2.50 and half dollar.

These two are common overall but rare and elusive in gem 65 and above. An odd coincidence, if you ask me. Both coins are very popular.

Commemoratives are often of interest to collectors whose state issued the coin, particularly states with large populations like California, Texas and New York. There is substantial demand among non-traditional coin buyers for commemoratives based on historical and regional considerations.

Thus, the market for commemorative issues is broad and with good reason. Unlike traditional single-issue sets, they offer more than 100 portraits of Americana, five denominations in two metals and a span of seven decades. No wonder this series attracts buyers across the spectrum, both here and abroad.

The Market

Wholesale commemorative values are available to anyone with the price of a subscription to the *Coin Dealer Newsletter* or the *Certified Coin Dealer Newsletter*. In the trade these are referred to as the *Graysheet* and *Bluesheet*, which represents the color paper they are printed on. The *Graysheet* has been around since 1963 and is the most successful publication of its kind. It tracks the values of sight-seen dealer transactions as well as coins that do not lend themselves to certification. The *Bluesheet*, an outgrowth of certification, was begun in 1986 to track and record the value of certified coins by grading service. Its values are meant to represent the sight-unseen levels.*

The folks that publish these data study the electronic trading exchanges for commemorative values. They also get information from auctions and offline dealer-to-dealer transactions. However, due to easy accessibility and recording, electronic exchanges appear to provide the majority of data, especially for the *Bluesheet*. There are currently two exchanges (Certified Coin Network and Certified Coin Exchange). Dealers place bids for coins by grading service and qualify that bid as sight seen or sight unseen. Although both exchanges allow the posting of bids for ANACS coins and one exchange even has a slot for uncertified examples, PCGS and NGC coins account for nearly all transactions. Additionally, both exchanges allow the posting of "asks" (offers to sell a coin) but ask transactions are infrequent and represent only a small percentage of total transactions. Bidding dominates these systems and the number of sight-unseen and sight-seen bids seems to be about equal.

Certification was a giant step toward standardization of rare coins. It did not, however, make all coins equal. Two MS64 Vancouvers in PCGS holders are not always worth the same price unless the coins have extremely similar characteristics. Let me explain. Even within the same grade and grading service, eye appeal can differ. Some coins are high end for the grade, some in the middle and some low end. Sight-unseen bids placed on the exchange represent the low end of the market while sight bids represent the high end. Coins in the middle are represented by the spreads between the two bids.

The publishers of the *Bluesheet/Graysheet* attempt to represent this spread using the *Bluesheet* for unseen prices and the *Graysheet* for sight values. Several factors, some beyond their control, keep them from succeeding completely. First, as mentioned before, they do not list every issue individually, even though dealers trade them this way. Grouping PDS sets under one price leads to inaccuracies and misunderstandings. Second, several grades in the *Bluesheet* are not included in the *Graysheet*, most notably MS62, 66 and 67. Perhaps the solution is a monthly supplemental listing to both sheets of all issues in all grades. Such a page is currently available for P/L Morgan dollars, Standing Liberty quarters and St. Gaudens $20 gold pieces among others.

Another problem facing the *Bluesheet* and *Graysheet* is the sheer size and diversity of the market. Sometimes price inconsistencies develop. It is common to find examples in the *Bluesheet* and *Graysheet* that have the same or nearly the same value on issues where a spread actually exists in the marketplace. Some data are harder to retrieve than other data. Inaccuracies through omission are not uncommon.

---

* *A sight-seen (or "sight") bid means the dealer must view the coin and approve it before the transaction is complete. A sight-unseen bid means the dealer commits to buying the coin in the grade and holder specified regardless of its appearance.*

The major problem in regard to the sheets revolves around interpretation. The *Graysheet* reports higher prices but does not clearly indicate that it too applies to certified coins. The *Bluesheet*, on the other hand, does not emphasize that its prices represent the low end of the market. Customers and dealers try to use the sheets to their own advantage. Stealthy buyers try to purchase nice sight-quality examples at (*Bluesheet*) sight-unseen prices. This is frustrating for dealers whose costs are rooted in sight levels.

For example, most of the coins I purchase for our customers are sight quality. We pay around the sight levels, often without consulting the *Bluesheet*. As a subscriber to both national teletype services and perhaps the most prolific bidder on commemoratives, my buy prices are more likely to reflect the prices listed on the exchange than those in the *Bluesheet*. Reasonable and experienced customers, as well as dealers, understand these differences and accept that values of nice specimens are more accurately reflected in the *Graysheet* or at some additional percentage to *Bluesheet* values.

PCGS versus NGC

The Professional Coin Grading Service (PCGS) was originally started by seven coin dealers in 1986 to standardize rare coin grading. Borrowing heavily from David Hall's cash market program,[*] this concept revolutionized the way rare coins were traded. PCGS became the leading third-party grading service, a position it still holds today. One of the original seven was a dealer named John Albanese who split from the others to form his own grading service the next year called Numismatic Guaranty Corporation (NGC).

Generally speaking, PCGS coins are somewhat more valuable than NGC coins in the same grade.

There are several reasons for this. PCGS garnered a large market share, with significant dealer support and participation, before NGC opened its doors. Additionally, NGC had a greater tendency in the beginning to grade heavily encrusted and toned coins more favorably than PCGS. Although these coins had been popular among experienced numismatists in the 1970's and early 1980's, tastes were changing and buyers were more interested in eye appeal than technical grades based on originality. With a larger base and a larger budget, PCGS continued to enjoy advantages over NGC even though the quality of their products became similar.

On lower-price, sight-quality coins, you can expect to pay about the same with a small edge going to PCGS. On more expensive issues, sight-quality PCGS coins can sell for up to 20% more than NGC. The average difference is usually around 10% depending on the issue. It's easy to get two opinions as to which grading service is best. Because of higher values and greater market share, many choose PCGS. Contrary to this, some dealers tout NGC coins as a better buy because you can get the same coin for less money. Even if this were true, as it sometimes may be, it is probably irrelevant and the services are more similar than different. If you pay less than an equivalent PCGS coin cost then you will probably have to sell it for an equivalently lower amount. The in-and-out costs should be approximately the same.

Low-end (sight unseen) NGC coins can trade for even larger discounts owing to a lack of sight-unseen bidders for their product on the electronic networks. The NGC market suffers from a lack of support in this area. However, these lower sight-unseen bids can often lead to favorable prices on middle-quality coins. Even though NGC coins cost a little less than PCGS coins, they probably represent equivalent value on these pieces. As pointed out recently by Mark Salzberg of NGC in an article he wrote for *Coin World*, "Consumers should buy the coin not the holder." I agree – consumers should consider the coin's quality above whether it's in a PCGS or NGC holder. It should be mentioned that other grading services have not received the same level of acceptance as PCGS and NGC. Coins purchased in other holders must be evaluated on a case-by-case basis.

---

[*] *The cash market was David Hall's marketing program prior to PCGS. Coins were graded and placed into round, protective holders the size of the coin (Kointains®). They were then heat-sealed into 2.5" square flips with their grading label. Hall made cash buy/sell spreads on the issues he sold. The company guaranteed to repurchase these coins at the labeled grade as long as they remained in his holders. This method was adapted and became PCGS, of which David Hall is currently CEO.*

Can Coin Prices Rebound?

Commemoratives, like all areas of the coin market, have been in a five-year downtrend. Since the glorious 1989 peaks, coins have continued to move lower and lower with only a few minor upturns. None of these were significant and none lasted more than a few months. In 5 years, some prices declined almost 90% and many by 50%. Many coin buyers took a bath on their holdings.

Can coin prices rebound? Have populations grown too large? Were 1989 levels real or artificial? The answers to these questions can be obtained by a thorough examination of what has happened since 1986 and the beginnings of the rare coin revolution. The concept of coin standardization was long overdue. ANACS' photo certification had gained rapid and widespread popularity in the middle 1980's. Unfortunately, this service was unable to sustain its market share because of grading inconsistencies, inadequate dealer support and the lack of a tamper-proof protective holder. PCGS was able to almost immediately overcome these problems and its product was an instant success.

Coin prices rose in 1986 and again in 1989. These run-ups were due in some measure to the limited supply of coins in holders. This was demonstrated quite clearly by the 1989 market, where issues that appreciated the most were those with low populations. These are the same coins that suffered major declines as the bear market of the 1990's began to unwind. Now that populations have grown substantially, values are more in the line with reality. Many prices have reverted back to late 1970's and early 1980's levels, long before slabs were introduced. Nine years into the revolution of third party grading, prices have come full circle and the stage has been set for future growth.

An Even Playing Field

The most important change to rare coins as a result of certification was the tremendous increase in fairness. With impartial third parties doing the grading, dealers could no longer buy coins at one grade and sell them at another, a common practice before 1986. In addition, to the dismay of many dealers, profit margins declined dramatically. One dealer could not claim his MS65 was much different from another dealer's and a pattern of unfettered competition began. Information became more accessible and accurate as bids were posted on electronic trading circuits and population statistics were kept. Consumers had finally arrived on an even playing field and coin dealers would have to work hard and become more sophisticated to prosper.

Changes like these, that protect the consumer, usually occur when an industry is ready to go mainstream, but many dealers resisted. I have heard some dealers complaining and wishing for the old days, when the game was really one sided and they could make an easy buck. They prefer less information to more and try to blame their problems on coin certification or the recording of bids via electronic bidding centers. This is a classic case of shooting the messenger. Though these dealers can give multiple reasons why they feel the recording and dissemination of bids is wrong, their real but unspoken reason is that it makes the playing field too even. Left to this faction, censorship and deception would still be the name of the game.

Electronic bidding has propelled the coin industry into the 21st century. It has given the market much needed liquidity, confidence and accountability. Without these electronic bids, consumers cashing in their holdings would have to settle for a lower percentage of actual value. Even honest dealers, uncertain of what coins might bring, would leave themselves a larger cushion than necessary. Bids also eliminate a dealer's cash flow from negatively impacting on a transaction. Coins can be wholesaled more easily and even a dealer with a small capital base can make a sizable transaction. The existence of standing bids has given consumers and dealers more confidence to enter the market. I have often argued that buying coins is the secondary purpose of electronic bidding. The first is to display our demand, clearly, for all participants to see.

Bidding for certified coins on exchanges with rules is a good tool to keep dealers and price levels honest. The exchange makes dealers more accountable to other dealers as well as consumers. Before certification and electronic bids, a dealer requesting a certain item would advertise a bid in the general marketplace. Since coins were uncertified he had much more latitude to accept or decline the coin he was sent. In addition, he wasn't trading on an exchange and dealers tendering coins to him had little leverage to make him honor his bid. Bidding dealers often bought coins only when they were undergraded or when their closest buddies had some to sell. The "good old boy" network was the rule of the day. It was difficult for the average consumer or (unconnected) dealer to realize the bid price or even close to it. If you were not an insider you would have had to run a gauntlet of middle men. Now with a certified coin and a formal bid mechanism, anyone can participate and at levels much closer to the top.

I believe the widespread reporting of bids and the certification of rare coins has been our salvation and legitimized our market to a greater degree than ever before. This was nothing less than a complete turnaround from the free-for-all, let-the-buyers-beware attitude that preceded it. The new business climate ultimately led to a shakeout and realignment of the firms that constitute our industry. Today's successful dealer, besides having numismatic knowledge, is a sophisticated businessman who is equipped to make a profit on smaller margins, through higher volume, to the advantage of his customer. With certified coins, buy/sell spreads are much closer than ever before.

The Future

The 1990's is the age of the information highway and the coin business is rapidly entering. With increased reliance on computers and a fair playing field, demand for the numismatic product will continue to build. What was once a cottage industry with a cult-like following is attracting serious new investors with money to spend. There were not many safe places in the coin market for investors prior to 1986. Unfortunately, those that followed the rare coin revolution were hurt by the overblown bull markets of 1986 and 1989, but I think 1994 is different.

Several factors are occurring that could propel us to real, sustainable growth. Prices have decreased as populations increased so that future growth will only come through real demand. Price manipulations, which ultimately drive people from the market, are more difficult today and unlikely. Third-party grading combined with accessible information have made the coin market safer for a larger audience.

While these issues pertain primarily to the demand side of the equation, the unknown variable is still supply. As the populations have increased so have the percentages of the original mintages which have been certified. At some point, raw supply coming on to the market will greatly diminish and the number of coins coming into the certified market will slow down and eventually become a trickle.

Nobody can predict when this trend will become significant enough to affect prices. At that time, the other factors that have been set in place by certification and its trail of information will combine with lower production to create higher values. When this happens, I think commemoratives will be in the forefront. In the long run, today's buyers should be handsomely rewarded.

Chapter 3

THE SILVER COMMEMORATIVES

Isabella
Quarter – 1893

Mintage
Business strikes: 24,214
Ranking: (99)

Certified Populations & Historical Values

	MS60	MS62	MS63	MS64	MS65	MS66	MS67
Pop.	45	606	919	889	337	116	23
Rank	(140)	(141)	(132)	(99)	(47)	(74)	(100)
Pricing							
1957	—	—	$ 30	—	—	—	—
1970	—	—	70	—	—	—	—
1980	$ 475	—	675	—	$ 1,075	—	—
1982	320	—	550	—	1,200	$ 2,100	—
1989	345	$ 550	900	$ 2,000	5,750	10,900	$ 15,650
1994	265	325	480	755	1,625	3,500	7,500

Percent of mintage certified..13%
Popular collector grades...............................MS60-64 Popular investor grades................................MS64-67
Background: Issued as a souvenir for the Columbian Exposition – 400th anniversary celebration

Comments

The Isabella is the only quarter in this series. In addition, it is one of the earliest commems and is considered by many to have a beautiful and historic design. Isabellas are in strong demand by collectors right up to grade 65. Price declines over the last several years have made this coin appear cheap, especially in grades 64 to 66. It's probably no coincidence that the largest price drops are in the grades with the highest rankings. Certified populations were considerably lower in 1989 and limited supply may have been more of a factor than demand. This issue usually comes with toning due to prevailing storage and packaging of the day. When available, frosty white coins in any grade will sell quickly. Lightly toned coins are also desirable. When buying toned specimens, always try to determine if they are original and eye appealing. If a toned coin doesn't meet both these criteria, keep looking. Coins with vibrant, multicolored toning do exist in this issue; expect to pay a premium for them.

Even though price declines are the smallest in grades 60 to 63, current prices should be considered low. Strong collector demand exists for these grades. Specimens in 64 are sought by both collectors and investors and represent good value at today's levels. MS65 and 66 examples have experienced massive declines in recent years. Current prices seem to be appropriate and upside potential is greater than downside.

- ✓ Be careful when buying this coin sight unseen.
- ✓ Avoid baggy specimens or those with too many cuts.
- ✓ Avoid dark or splotchy toned coins from this issue.
- ✓ Author's choice: *Collector* MS64; *Investor* MS65. This issue is Highly Recommended.

Lafayette
Dollar – 1900

Mintage
Business strikes: 36,026
Ranking: (111)

Certified Populations & Historical Values

	MS60	MS62	MS63	MS64	MS65	MS66	MS67
Pop.	60	338	449	415	152	20	5
Rank	(141)	(135)	(109)	(60)	(19)	(24)	(57)
Pricing							
1957	—	—	$ 42	—	—	—	—
1970	—	—	165	—	—	—	—
1980	$ 1,600	—	2,500	—	$ 6,000	—	—
1982	525	—	1,050	—	3,500	$ 5,250	—
1989	600	$ 850	2,550	$ 7,800	18,250	31,750	$ 51,000
1994	480	650	1,420	2,625	7,000	12,000	70,000

Percent of mintage certified..6%
Popular collector grades...MS60-64 Popular investor grades..MS64-66
Background: Issued to raise money for a statue of Lafayette in Paris

Comments

The Lafayette dollar is the only dollar coin in this series. Because of this and its significant historical meaning the coin enjoys a strong demand function. Lafayette dollars in 60-62 especially white ones are always in demand by collectors. As a dealer I would purchase duplicates in these grades as long as they had decent eye appeal. MS63 and MS64 coins are sought by advanced collectors. The population of Lafayette dollars peaks in grade 63 so these coins are generally available. Although the population of 64's is similar to 63's the ranking rises significantly, making 64's considerably tougher. This trend continues to 65 and 66 where the Lafayette dollar is one of the scarcest non-PDS issues. The middle grades, especially 63 and 64 are also likely to be resubmitted so its not unusual to find fully graded to slightly overgraded coins. Expect to pay a premium for above average coins in these grades.

Coins which grade MS65 and better are usually purchased by investors but because commems are so heavily collected, a portion of these high grade specimens are also bought by collectors. White coins are rare above 64 but do exist. I recently purchased a blazing white gem 66 with a thick, frosty skin. A coin like this is a thing of beauty and worth every bit of its five-figure price. Coins with appealing toning or multicolored toning are also desirable in these higher grades since this is how original specimens come. Low grade mint state examples sell quickly and could probably support higher prices. Midrange coins are appropriately priced and come onto and go off the market at a consistent pace.

- ✓ Expect to pay a premium for PQ coins in this issue.
- ✓ Beware of excessive reed marks.
- ✓ Several varieties exist, see Swiatek.
- ✓ Author's choice: *Collector* MS64; *Investor* MS65. This issue is Highly Recommended.

Harry Laibstain

Alabama
1921

Mintage
Business strikes: 59,038
Ranking: (115)

Certified Populations & Historical Values

	MS60	MS62	MS63	MS64	MS65	MS66	MS67
Pop.	14	166	484	694	149	5	0
Rank	(125)	(121)	(113)	(95)	(18)	(6)	(1)
Pricing							
1957	—	—	$ 40	—	—	—	—
1970	—	—	42	—	—	—	—
1980	$ 350	—	500	—	$ 875	—	—
1982	210	—	365	—	825	$ 1,650	—
1989	180	$ 250	500	$ 4,100	10,000	27,500	$ 31,100
1994	160	285	475	815	2,720	8,000	15,500

Percent of mintage certified...3%
Popular collector grades...................................MS62-64 Popular investor grades...................................MS64-65
Background: Commemorate 1919 centennial of statehood

Comments

The Alabama is one of several early issues from the 1920's. Many have been circulated or mishandled and the number of certifiable mint state coins available is low. Only 3% of this issue has been certified mint state. The rarity of this coin is similar to its sister, the 2x2, which has a much lower mintage. Compared to the 2x2 it's rarer in higher grades and more common in the lower grades. Although available up to MS64, Alabamas are very scarce in 65 and 66. Its certified population rankings of 18 in MS65 and 6 in MS66 are equivalent to 5th and 3rd when PDS issues are excluded (see *Tables 5 & 6*).

Alabamas are popular in all grades up to 65 but most of the action is in 63 and 64 coins where the population peaks. I like MS64's in this issue because their cost is not much more than 63's and way under 65's. Although 65's seem expensive, it's interesting to note that they are about one-fourth of what they were at their peak in 1989. Low supply and steady demand keep this issue firm. A look at the 64 column will provide an even greater contrast as the 1994 price compared to 1989 is 1 to 5. Grades 63 and below have strong demand from collectors and prices here are solid as well.

- ✓ Hard to find without some facial friction (obverse) and striking problems (reverse).
- ✓ Coins with very good luster are available; avoid dull or spotted coins.
- ✓ Large spreads over the years have made this coin subject to numerous regrades. Beware of washed-out or toned-over specimens.
- ✓ Author's choice: *Collector* MS63; *Investor* MS64. This issue is Highly Recommended.

Alabama 2x2
1921

Mintage
Business strikes: 6,006
Ranking: (42)

Certified Populations & Historical Values

	MS60	MS62	MS63	MS64	MS65	MS66	MS67
Pop.	9	188	433	584	176	12	1
Rank	(118)	(126)	(108)	(88)	(24)	(15)	(27)
Pricing							
1957	—	—	$ 45	—	—	—	—
1970	—	—	60	—	—	—	—
1980	$ 425	—	650	—	$ 1,200	—	—
1982	275	—	435	—	1,050	$ 1,850	—
1989	240	$ 320	600	$ 4,175	9,500	25,000	$30,500
1994	230	365	540	910	2,720	8,000	20,000

Percent of mintage certified..24%
Popular collector grades..MS60-64   Popular investor grades...................................MS64-65
Background: 2x2 added to indicate 22nd state

Comments

The design of the Alabama 2x2 differs from the plain only by the addition of a 2x2 in the right obverse field. The mintage is almost 1/10th that of the regular Alabama but today the rarities are similar. Both coins have population rankings over 100 in grades 60-63 and become noticeably scarcer above this level. The 2x2's rankings of 24th and 15th in MS65 and MS66 rise to 7th and 5th when PDS issues are excluded.

These coins enjoy different types of demand which, ironically, keep them relatively similar. The Alabama "plain" is part of the 50-piece type set and is most often included by collectors. The 2x2 has a low mintage that tends to attract the hoarders and collector/investor types who believe mintage will eventually determine rarity. These buyers tend to buy more than one example. I know of at least one collector who has more than 50 pieces of this issue in mint state.

Although the percent certified is high, I do not believe the rarity relationship of this coin to the plain will change. In fact, the evidence suggests just the opposite. It seems that collectors who bought 2x2's intended to keep and preserve them because they were a special variety of a more general collectible coin. It stands to reason that a larger percentage of these survive in mint state today. I feel it's as likely that a mini-hoard of 2x2 gems would come out as a group of plains. Prices below 65 are strongly supported by collectors and hoarders. MS65 and higher specimens are mainly demanded by investors and, as long as supply stays relatively low, price levels should remain firm.

TIPS!
- ✓ 2x2's can be found with thick fresh luster.
- ✓ Don't hesitate to pay a premium for nice quality coins.
- ✓ Avoid coins with any deep cuts or excessive chatter.
- ✓ Author's choice: *Collector* MS63; *Investor* MS64. This coin is Highly Recommended.

Harry Laibstain

Albany
1936

Mintage
Business strikes: 17,671
Ranking: (92)

Certified Populations & Historical Values

	MS60	MS62	MS63	MS64	MS65	MS66	MS67
Pop.	1	91	524	1,533	1,336	419	53
Rank	(66)	(111)	(117)	(129)	(133)	(128)	(123)
Pricing							
1957	—	—	$ 20	—	—	—	—
1970	—	—	42	—	—	—	—
1980	$ 275	—	350	—	$ 550	—	—
1982	165	—	210	—	340	$ 680	—
1989	260	$ 270	325	$ 675	1,525	4,850	$ 8,400
1994	185	190	200	250	540	910	2,600

Percent of mintage certified..22%
Popular collector grades.................................MS64-65 Popular investor grades................................MS65-66
Background: 250th anniversary of the charter of Albany, New York

Comments

Despite a mintage below 20,000, the Albany is relatively common in all grades. The population peaks in MS64 with a strong lean to 65. All population rankings from 64 on are above 120. Albanys have a high basal value and its influence can be seen up to grade 64. Whether collecting or investing, I only recommend the purchase of coins grading MS64 or higher.

Albanys often come with lustrous white surfaces. Currently these are the most desirable coins, excluding the small number of vibrant multicolor toned coins. Unfortunately, the design of the Albany lends itself to several quality problems. Most troublesome is the beaver's rump and hind leg, which often show friction and can be flattened or scraped. I recently saw an MS67 where this area was heavily frictioned. High-grade coins should not have significant problems in this area. Always inspect this trouble spot. It is also common for Albanys to have stainy toning or discoloration. These examples are unappealing and difficult to sell.

Below grade 65, prices are supported by collector demand and are relatively stable. Grades 65 and above appear to be fully priced despite significant drops since 1989. These grades would benefit greatly from some increase in demand. Even a small increase could translate to price growth, particularly in MS66.

- ✓ Watch out for coins with heavy bag marks.
- ✓ Expect to find some friction or album slide lines on the beaver.
- ✓ Avoid mottled toning or washed-out coins from this issue.
- ✓ Author's choice: *Collector* MS64; *Investor* MS66.

Antietam
1937

Mintage
Business strikes: 18,028
Ranking: (93)

Certified Populations & Historical Values

	MS60	MS62	MS63	MS64	MS65	MS66	MS67
Pop.	2	52	327	1,035	1,387	538	116
Rank	(93)	(97)	(97)	(109)	(136)	(135)	(136)
Pricing							
1957	—	—	$ 32	—	—	—	—
1970	—	—	72	—	—	—	—
1980	$ 350	—	500	—	$ 775	—	—
1982	225	—	300	—	465	$ 950	—
1989	375	$ 440	485	$ 575	1,250	3,725	$ 5,000
1994	340	345	365	400	520	895	1,750

Percent of mintage certified..19%
Popular collector grades...MS64-66 Popular investor grades...MS65-67
Background: 75th anniversary of this Civil War battle

Comments

Antietams are a very popular issue. One of four Civil War issues, they are often collected as a subset or as part of the 50-piece type set. Antietams come extremely nice, some with incredible white blazing luster and others with exciting toning. Their population peaks in MS65, which puts them right up there with the highest quality commems. The "bad news" is that these coins are not scarce in high grade. Certified population rankings of 136, 135 and 136 in grades MS65 to MS67 attest to this. With almost 20% of the mintage certified, gems abound.

This is one of those coins that MS65 collectors often buy in 66 because the premium is relatively small. I remember buying an MS66 Antietam for $3,650 just before the Long Beach show in 1989 and selling it for the then-current bid of $3,700. I realized immediately how lucky I was because the rarity did not support the price. At today's $895 it's considerably more reasonable.

Prices for coins graded 60 to 64 are supported by this issue's high basal value. MS65 coins carry only a small premium over MS64 and represent a good value for the collector. This is a high demand issue throughout the grade range.

- ✓ Do not buy this coin below MS65.
- ✓ Avoid coins with excessive or heavy marks.
- ✓ White coins should have strong vibrant original luster. Toned coins should be pretty.
- ✓ Author's choice: *Collector* MS65; *Investor* MS66. This issue is Recommended.

Harry Laibstain

Arkansas
1935-P, D, S

Mintage
Business strikes: 13012, 5505, 5506
Ranking: (85) (31) (34)

Certified Populations & Historical Values

	MS60	MS62	MS63	MS64	MS65	MS66	MS67
35-P: Pop	1	48	301	644	361	31	3
Rank	(66)	(93)	(94)	(93)	(52)	(36)	(47)
35-D: Pop	2	22	163	423	319	67	7
Rank	(93)	(69)	(74)	(61)	(43)	(55)	(65)
35-S: Pop	0	33	181	433	333	60	3
Rank	(1)	(83)	(75)	(63)	(46)	(53)	(47)
Set Pricing							
1957	—	—	$ 6	—	—	—	—
1970	—	—	35	—	—	—	—
1980	$ 225	—	275	—	$ 400	—	—
1982	210	—	260	—	425	$ 850	—
1989	225	$ 265	300	$1,275	4,350	10,800	$25,350
1994	207	207	210	270	1,075	3,720	21,000
Individual Pricing (1994)							
1935-P	$ 69	$ 69	$ 70	$ 90	$ 360	$ 1,240	—
1935-D	69	69	70	90	360	1,240	—
1935-S	69	69	70	90	360	1,240	—

Percent of mintage certified...11%, 10%, 19%
Popular collector grades.................................MS63-65 Popular investor grades......................................MS64-66
Background: 100th anniversary of Arkansas' admission to the Union

Comments

All 1935 Arkansas commems are common dates and are represented by type prices. Although the 1935-P has both a higher mintage and a higher population, it trades on par with the slightly scarcer '35-D and S. The Arkansas design lends itself to several quality problems. The most common is nicked or hairlined obverses. The coins are so open on the obverse that it's hard to find coins with clean cheeks and frosty fields. The second problem, encountered less often, is the eagle's strike on the reverse. Coins seem to run the gamut from a full, sharp strike to a flat one. Ironically, many of the coins with clean obverses and clean fields have weak strikes.

Expect to pay a premium for nice white coins with clean frosty cheeks. Coins with light, even toning are also in demand. Arkansas prices are heavily represented by their basal value in grades up to MS63. Significant price declines in recent years in MS64 and MS65 make these coins attractive and fairly priced.

- ✓ Avoid dark or spotty toning on these issues.
- ✓ Matched sets usually command a small premium.
- ✓ Grade Arkansas more heavily by obverse surfaces.
- ✓ Author's choice: *Collector* MS64; *Investor* MS65. This issue is Recommended.

Arkansas
1936-P, D, S

Mintage
Business strikes: 9660, 9660, 9662
Ranking: (65) (65) (67)

Certified Populations & Historical Values

	MS60	MS62	MS63	MS64	MS65	MS66	MS67
36-P: Pop	1	60	277	472	193	23	2
Rank	(66)	(102)	(90)	(70)	(28)	(28)	(44)
36-D: Pop	4	33	289	546	297	39	8
Rank	(109)	(83)	(92)	(79)	(41)	(44)	(69)
36-S: Pop	4	40	249	501	294	42	4
Rank	(109)	(90)	(88)	(73)	(39)	(45)	(54)
Set Pricing							
1957	—	—	$ 16	—	—	—	—
1970	—	—	34	—	—	—	—
1980	$ 225	—	275	—	$ 400	—	—
1982	210	—	260	—	425	$ 850	—
1989	225	$ 265	300	$ 1,275	4,350	10,800	$25,350
1994	207	207	210	270	*1,200	3,720	21,000
Individual Pricing (1994)							
1936-P	$ 69	$ 69	$ 70	$ 90	$ 400	$ 1,240	—
1936-D	69	69	70	90	350	1,240	—
1936-S	69	69	70	90	350	1,240	—

Percent of mintage certified..11%, 13%, 12%
Popular collector grades.........................MS63-65 Popular investor grades...................................MS64-66
Background: 100th anniversary of Arkansas' admission to the Union

Comments

More Arkansas commems were minted in 1936 than any other year and all 1936 issues sell as common dates, with the exception of '36-P in MS65. With a population of just 193, it is scarcer than all three 1935 Arkansas, both of its sister coins and the '37-D, which currently carries a small premium. This coin is often offered as type and most dealers do not recognize its premium value. The '36 design is identical to the '35's and the same description and information apply (see notes on 1935 Arkansas).

Arkansas' prices have declined a great deal since the 1989 peaks. Like most PDS issues, their individual rarity has been overlooked. Most commemorative buyers focus either on the 50-piece type set or single-issue coins. It is somewhat ironic that collectors treat the commemorative series like type coins and purchase only one of each design. All other coin series from this period are collected by date and mintmark even though all issues share the same design. Prices in 64 and 65 seem low at present.

✓ Current set pricing in MS65 indicates premium over common dates, which is not supported.
✓ Matched sets usually command a small premium.
✓ Expect to pay a premium for clean white coins or those with pretty multicolored toning. These issues do not normally come nice.
✓ Author's choice: *Collector* MS64; *Investor* MS65. This PDS set is Recommended.

Harry Laibstain

Arkansas
1937-P, D, S

Mintage
Business strikes: 5505, 5505, 5506
Ranking: (31) (31) (34)

Certified Populations & Historical Values

	MS60	MS62	MS63	MS64	MS65	MS66	MS67
37-P: Pop	1	32	233	382	160	22	0
Rank	(66)	(81)	(83)	(51)	(21)	(27)	(1)
37-D: Pop	1	21	192	399	233	33	3
Rank	(66)	(67)	(77)	(56)	(35)	(39)	(47)
37-S: Pop	1	43	192	353	106	14	1
Rank	(66)	(92)	(77)	(44)	(6)	(17)	(27)
Set Pricing							
1957	—	—	$ 22	—	—	—	—
1970	—	—	34	—	—	—	—
1980	$ 250	—	300	—	$ 450	—	—
1982	220	—	275	—	460	$ 920	—
1989	225	$ 265	300	$ 1,300	4,350	10,800	$ 25,500
1994	207	210	240	285	1,375	*5,100	21,000
Individual Pricing (1994)							
1937-P	$ 69	$ 70	$ 80	$ 95	$ 450	$ 1,500	—
1937-D	69	70	80	95	425	1,375	—
1937-S	69	70	80	95	500	2,000	—

Percent of mintage certified...15%, 16%, 13%
Popular collector grades...MS64-65 Popular investor grades...MS65-66
Background: 100th anniversary of Arkansas' admission to the Union

Comments

A new trend began for the Arkansas in 1937 — declining mintages. Perhaps interest in the issue was waning. This is ironic because, today, this is where the Arkansas sets get interesting. The certified ranking of 21st, 35th and 6th, respectively, make this a tough set to put together in 65.

All three issues carry a premium in this grade with the S being the most valuable. The D carries a small premium and can usually be counted on for the highest quality in this set. The P mint also comes fairly nice and carries a moderate premium. All 3 coins are underrated in MS65. Average quality MS64 coins carry little or no premium. This was not always the case. During the late '80's the P and S carried a 30-50% premium over common type prices. As prices rose into 1989, most of the premiums dissolved. When prices declined, the premiums never reappeared, probably due to the increasing certified populations of these issues.

Coins that are PQ for the grade in 64 may command a premium. Since the MS65 prices are 4 to 5 times MS64 prices, nice 64's are likely to grab a piece of the spread. MS66 issues carry a premium of the same order as 65 issues. See 1935 and 1936 sets for more information pertaining to the Arkansas issue.

✓ The S mint in this set does not come nice. Be prepared to pay a premium for nice coins.
✓ 1937 sets in MS65 have excellent investment potential.
✓ Avoid coins with reed marks or heavy cuts.
✓ Author's choice: *Collector* MS64; *Investor* MS65. This issue is Highly Recommended.

TIPS!

Arkansas
1938-P, D, S

Mintage
Business strikes: 3156, 3155, 3156
Ranking: (15) (14) (15)

Certified Populations & Historical Values

	MS60	MS62	MS63	MS64	MS65	MS66	MS67
38-P: Pop	0	23	143	237	116	13	1
Rank	(1)	(72)	(65)	(21)	(9)	(16)	(27)
38-D: Pop	0	31	125	229	143	27	5
Rank	(1)	(78)	(56)	(19)	(16)	(32)	(57)
38-S: Pop	1	33	141	224	108	8	1
Rank	(66)	(83)	(64)	(17)	(7)	(11)	(27)
Set Pricing							
1957	—	—	$ 55	—	—	—	—
1970	—	—	51	—	—	—	—
1980	$ 475	—	600	—	$ 950	—	—
1982	365	—	485	—	925	$ 1,850	—
1989	395	$ 440	475	$ 1,650	4,550	10,800	$ 27,500
1994	260	315	350	550	1,875	*6,550	24,750
Individual Pricing (1994)							
1938-P	$ 87	$ 105	$ 117	$ 183	$ 650	$ 2,250	—
1938-D	87	105	117	183	525	1,500	—
1938-S	87	105	117	183	700	2,250	—

Percent of mintage certified..................17%, 18%, 16%
Popular collector grades.........MS63-64   Popular investor grades.........MS65-66
Background: 100th anniversary of Arkansas' admission to the Union

Comments

With mintage and population rankings all falling into the top 20, this issue is genuinely scarce. The 1938 Arkansas do not trade as type in any grade. Currently, 65 prices are about right although moderately underrated. Nice '38 Arkansas in MS65 sell almost immediately at current levels. The interesting thing about this set is the extremely low prices of 63 and 64 coins. While I would not usually recommend these lower grades for investors, they are a bargain for the budget-conscious collector. Do not overlook the large spreads between 64 and 65 and be prepared to pay a premium for above-average coins in 64. If I were building a 50-piece type set, I would use one of these instead of a 1935 or 1936 issue.

Like 1937 Arks, the S mint does not come nice as evidenced by its low population and high ranking. Buy all the nice S mints in 65 you can (see '35 Arkansas sets for a more complete description of problem areas in the design).

Price declines on the rarer PDS issues have not been as large as declines on single-issue coins. This does not mean they don't have the same or greater potential for growth. In fact, as stated previously, I feel these better date PDS issues have been overlooked. Actual supply is small, and if demand were to increase, prices would respond quickly.

✓ Mintages and pops on these coins can be misleading as this issue is subject to hoarding.
✓ 1938 sets represent good investment potential in grades 64 to 66.
✓ Matched sets and sets with pretty toning are available. Expect to pay a premium.
✓ Author's choice: *Collector* MS64; *Investor* MS65. This issue is <u>Highly Recommended</u>.

Harry Laibstain

Arkansas
1939-P, D, S

Mintage
Business strikes: 2104, 2104, 2104
Ranking: (6)   (6)   (6)

Certified Populations & Historical Values

	MS60	MS62	MS63	MS64	MS65	MS66	MS67
39-P: Pop	1	32	133	204	84	5	0
Rank	(66)	(81)	(61)	(10)	(1)	(6)	(1)
39-D: Pop	1	22	116	201	119	21	1
Rank	(66)	(69)	(51)	(9)	(10)	(26)	(27)
39-S: Pop	0	30	103	187	145	15	1
Rank	(1)	(76)	(46)	(6)	(17)	(20)	(27)
Set Pricing							
1957	—	—	$ 160	—	—	—	—
1970	—	—	270	—	—	—	—
1980	$ 1,350	—	1,600	—	$2,050	—	—
1982	750	—	1,000	—	1,600	$ 2,800	—
1989	750	$ 825	900	$ 2,400	8,000	16,050	$ 30,500
1994	600	660	675	900	2,310	*7,850	25,500
Individual Pricing (1994)							
1939-P	$ 200	$ 220	$ 225	$ 300	$ 850	$ 3,000	—
1939-D	200	220	225	300	740	1,800	—
1939-S	200	220	225	300	720	1,800	—

Percent of mintage certified...22%, 23%, 23%
Popular collector grades...............................MS63-64 Popular investor grades.................................MS65-66
Background: 100th anniversary of Arkansas' admission to the Union

Comments

This is the king of the Arkansas sets. Like the '38's, the '39 set ranks in the top 20 in mintages and populations (for MS65). The only coins in the entire series with lower mintages are the '38 Boones and the '35/4-D and S overdate Boones. Many collectors and investors are initially attracted to these issues for this reason. Although mintage does not actually determine rarity, a low mintage creates an interest that spurs demand, creating a self-fulfilling prophesy or enhancing the rarity that's already there.

Of the three mints, the 1939-P is rarest in grades 65 and above, as it often has a steel/flat luster. In fact, the 1939-P is the rarest commemorative in 65, ranking No. 1 — ahead of single-coin issues thought to be much scarcer. Unlike the '37 and '38 sets, the S mint is the most common of the three (in MS65). I often see frosty gem quality S mints in 64 and 65 holders. The D mint is usually available with nice luster and a good strike.

1939 Arks that are white or attractively toned sell quickly at current levels and this set is one of my favorites. Because 1939 Arkansas have such low mintages, circulated and low mint state coins are not worth much less than higher, more collectible grades like MS63 and 64. I do not recommend the purchase of these coins below certified grade 63. Whenever you can get a big jump in quality for a small increase in price, take the quality.

- ✓ Low mintage set and subject to hoarding.
- ✓ 1939 sets represent good investment potential in grades 64 to 66.
- ✓ Avoid dark or spotted coins in this issue.
- ✓ Author's choice: *Collector* MS64; *Investor* MS65. This issue is Highly Recommended.

Bay Bridge
1936-S

Mintage
Business strikes: 71,424
Ranking: (119)

Certified Populations & Historical Values

	MS60	MS62	MS63	MS64	MS65	MS66	MS67
Pop.	16	173	679	1,471	1,314	420	59
Rank	(127)	(123)	(126)	(125)	(132)	(129)	(126)
Pricing							
1957	—	—	$ 11	—	—	—	—
1970	—	—	20	—	—	—	—
1980	$ 90	—	125	—	$ 235	—	—
1982	82	—	120	—	182	$ 365	—
1989	160	$ 170	175	$ 325	925	2,500	$ 3,000
1994	75	85	105	145	355	660	2,150

Percent of mintage certified..6%
Popular collector grades.............................MS63-64   Popular investor grades...............................MS65-66
Background: Commemorates opening of the San Francisco-Oakland Bay Bridge in California

Comments

The San Francisco Bay Bridge is popular for two reasons: the design is considered very attractive and it's a California issue. Even though the Bay Bridge is one of the most common commems, it moves off the market rapidly, especially in 63 and 64. White coins at these levels sell immediately. This coin is graded almost solely by its obverse. The reverse design is so busy that marks and changes in coloration are hard to detect. Bay Bridges come frosty white, however, undipped specimens with mark-free obverses are very hard to locate. The obverse of this coin is as unprotected from marks, scuffs and hairlines as the reverse is protected. Expect MS65 or MS66 coins to have some light ticks on the obverse. They should be clean but they will not be perfect. It is interesting to note that the population rankings are consistent across the grade range. This is a common issue but high demand tends to balance out high supply. Prices for grades 66 and below appear accurate, with lower-grade examples exhibiting some potential for growth.

✓ Avoid excessive ticks or heavy cuts on the bear.
✓ Popular California issue, scarcer than population indicates particularly in lower grades.
✓ Grade this coin by obverse.
✓ Author's choice: *Collector* MS64; *Investor* MS65.

TIPS!

Boone
1934

Mintage
Business strikes: 10,007
Ranking: (74)

Certified Populations & Historical Values

	MS60	MS62	MS63	MS64	MS65	MS66	MS67
Pop.	0	33	152	432	506	125	11
Rank	(1)	(83)	(70)	(62)	(77)	(77)	(74)
Pricing							
1957	—	—	$ 8	—	—	—	—
1970	—	—	16	—	—	—	—
1980	$ 103	—	130	—	$ 225	—	—
1982	100	—	140	—	245	$ 490	—
1989	100	$ 100	110	$ 210	700	1,525	$ 4,575
1994	70	75	80	90	140	418	2,000

Percent of mintage certified..13%
Popular collector grades.................................MS63-65   Popular investor grades...................................MS65-66
Background: 200th anniversary of Daniel Boone's birth

Comments

The 1934 Boone was the first year of this 16-coin multi-year set. It is the only Boone without a Denver or San Francisco counterpart. This coin trades as type in every grade and has the second highest mintage of all Boones. They are available brilliant in grades up to MS65. MS66 specimens usually come with light to moderate toning.

Boones are widely collected in MS64 and MS65. MS64 coins trade at only a slight premium over lower grades and represent a terrific quality vs. price play, especially on common dates like the 1934. With the price decline over the last several years, MS65 coins have become attractive to both collectors and investors. At current 65 levels, I like this type and recommend it. Investors should note a 5-to-1 drop since 1989.

✓ Desirable moderate rarity ranking of low-priced coin.
✓ Part of 16-piece sub-set within the commem set.
✓ Avoid stainy toning that sometimes plagues this issue.
✓ Author's choice: *Collector* MS64; *Investor* MS65. This issue is Recommended.

Boone
1935-P, D, S

Mintage
Business strikes: 10010, 5005, 5005
Ranking: (80) (22) (22)

Certified Populations & Historical Values

	MS60	MS62	MS63	MS64	MS65	MS66	MS67
35-P: Pop	2	31	245	542	503	112	14
Rank	(93)	(78)	(87)	(78)	(76)	(71)	(84)
35-D: Pop	0	15	137	370	236	87	3
Rank	(1)	(45)	(62)	(47)	(36)	(63)	(47)
35-S: Pop	0	17	108	283	417	177	11
Rank	(1)	(53)	(47)	(28)	(62)	(92)	(74)
Set Pricing							
1957	—	—	$ 5	—	—	—	—
1970	—	—	40	—	—	—	—
1980	$ 260	—	350	—	$ 550	—	—
1982	250	—	335	—	490	$ 980	—
1989	300	$ 320	330	$ 630	2,100	5,500	$10,800
1994	195	201	225	270	450	*1740	6,000
Individual Pricing (1994)							
1935-P	$ 65	$ 67	$ 75	$ 90	$ 150	$ 425	—
1935-D	65	67	75	90	150	550	—
1935-S	65	67	75	90	150	425	—

Percent of mintage certified..15%, 17%, 20%
Popular collector grades...............................MS64-65 Popular investor grades.................................MS65-66
Background: 200th anniversary of Daniel Boone's birth

Comments

The mintage of the '35-P is twice that of the D and S but the coins virtually all trade at type prices. A small premium is justified for the '35-D in MS65 and a moderate premium should be expected in 66. The D is harder to get in higher grades because the issue has some quality problems. 1935-D Boones are not always well struck and sometimes come baggy. The population chart shows an interesting trend as '35-D's are more common in 63 and 64 grades but less so in 65 and 66 than the 1935-S. This trend highlights the difference in production quality and handling between the two issues. Boones are available in white or lightly toned condition and represent excellent value in MS65. The high points on this issue are Daniel Boone's jaw, eye and forehead area. Look for scrapes and hairlining problems here.

✓ Matched sets, brilliant or toned, command a premium.
✓ White coins in 66 usually command a small premium.
✓ Current data on MS66 set prices may overstate actual value.
✓ Author's choice: *Collector* MS64; *Investor* MS65. This issue is Recommended.

Harry Laibstain

Boone
1935/34-P, D, S

Mintage
Business strikes: 10008, 2003, 2004
Ranking: (76) (1) (2)

Certified Populations & Historical Values

	MS60	MS62	MS63	MS64	MS65	MS66	MS67
35/4-P: Pop	0	28	198	579	561	153	7
Rank	(1)	(75)	(80)	(86)	(83)	(84)	(65)
35/4-D: Pop	0	14	67	161	181	87	16
Rank	(1)	(42)	(25)	(2)	(27)	(63)	(87)
35/4-S: Pop	0	17	77	189	177	50	3
Rank	(1)	(53)	(30)	(7)	(26)	(49)	(47)
Set Pricing							
1957	—	—	$ 180	—	—	—	—
1970	—	—	250	—	—	—	—
1980	$ 1,400	—	1,650	—	$ 1,950	—	—
1982	800	—	1,050	—	1,650	$ 2,900	—
1989	800	$ 850	900	$ 1,275	2,825	7,780	$11,200
1994	450	525	600	900	1,500	*3150	8,500
Individual Pricing (1994)							
35/4-P	$ 70	$ 75	$ 80	$ 90	$ 150	$ 400	—
35/4-D	190	225	260	405	690	875	—
35/4-S	190	225	260	405	660	1,150	—

Percent of mintage certified..15%, 27%, 26%
Popular collector grades..MS63-65 Popular investor grades..MS65-66
Background: 200th anniversary of Daniel Boone's birth

Comments

The '35/34 Boones or double dates resulted from the addition of the commemorative date, 1934, above the words "Pioneer year". The P-mint issue is a common Boone and trades as type in every grade. The D and S mints have the honor of being the lowest mintage coins of the entire 144-piece commem series and are hoarded for this reason. Although their MS65 ranking is high, they do not make the top 20.

The P is available in white or lightly toned condition up to grades 66. The D mint is available frosty white with a hard, unusual luster. Die polishing is often evident. Sometimes MS63 and 64 coins look gem but will not grade higher. The grading services tend to discount for the unusual surfaces even though this is how they come. They are more likely to grade lightly toned coins higher since toning camouflages the surfaces. The S mint has similar characteristics but is more often seen proof-like. Both grading services have trouble grading this coin.

This set is one of my favorites. Nice sets and mintmarked singles sell quickly. Note: To figure individual prices from a set price, subtract type value and divide the remainder by two. This will give you prices for the D and S. In MS66 the S commands a substantial premium over the D. Current listed set prices may overstate actual values.

- ✓ Beware of purchasing the P mint at 1/3 the price of the 3-piece set. It is a common type coin.
- ✓ Populations probably include many regrades since the coins often look better than they will grade.
- ✓ High basal values. Purchase only in grades 63 and above.
- ✓ Author's choice: *Collector* MS64; *Investor* MS65. This issue is Highly Recommended.

Boone
1936-P, D, S

Mintage
Business strikes: 12012, 5005, 5006
Ranking: (84) (22) (27)

Certified Populations & Historical Values

	MS60	MS62	MS63	MS64	MS65	MS66	MS67
36-P: Pop	1	51	231	658	676	184	21
Rank	(66)	(95)	(82)	(94)	(97)	(93)	(96)
36-D: Pop	0	16	122	414	471	109	8
Rank	(1)	(49)	(54)	(59)	(70)	(70)	(69)
36-S: Pop	0	15	124	320	435	185	21
Rank	(1)	(45)	(55)	(36)	(66)	(95)	(96)
Set Pricing							
1957	—	—	$ 4	—	—	—	—
1970	—	—	40	—	—	—	—
1980	$ 260	—	360	—	$ 550	—	—
1982	260	—	350	—	525	$ 1,050	—
1989	300	$ 320	330	$ 630	2,100	4,575	$10,800
1994	195	201	210	270	450	*1410	6,000
Individual Pricing (1994)							
1936-P	$ 65	$ 67	$ 70	$ 90	$ 150	$ 400	—
1936-D	65	67	70	90	150	475	—
1936-S	65	67	70	90	150	425	—

Percent of mintage certified...15%, 23%, 22%
Popular collector grades...............................MS64-65 Popular investor grades.................................MS65-66
Background: 200th anniversary of Daniel Boone's birth

Comments

The 1936 Boone set is similar in mintage and population to the 1935 set. Once again, the mintmarked issues are scarcer but do not trade for a premium. All 3 coins trade as type up to grade MS65. Only the '36-D develops any premium in grades above 65. The 1936 Boones generally come nice and are available as frosty white BU's. It is not unusual to see very thick-skinned, lightly toned gem BU examples. This would account for the higher population totals in grades MS65 and higher, compared to other Boone issues. These coins are not terribly rare but they are popular, sometimes collected as a set within a set.

✓ Should be able to find high-quality examples in this set.
✓ Do not pay a premium for these coins up to MS65.
✓ Matched sets or coins with pretty, colorful toning will command a moderate premium.
✓ Author's choice: *Collector* MS64; *Investor* MS65. This issue is Recommended.

Harry Laibstain

Boone
1937-P, D, S

Mintage
Business strikes: 9810, 2506, 2506
Ranking: (68) (9) (9)

Certified Populations & Historical Values

	MS60	MS62	MS63	MS64	MS65	MS66	MS67
37-P: Pop	1	33	199	580	643	186	25
Rank	(66)	(83)	(81)	(87)	(91)	(96)	(103)
37-D: Pop	0	9	74	211	231	79	21
Rank	(1)	(28)	(28)	(12)	(34)	(60)	(96)
37-S: Pop	0	14	69	167	212	72	11
Rank	(1)	(42)	(26)	(3)	(33)	(57)	(74)
Set Pricing							
1957	—	—	$ 150	—	—	—	—
1970	—	—	138	—	—	—	—
1980	$ 625	—	825	—	$ 1,100	—	—
1982	450	—	600	—	1,000	$ 2,000	—
1989	610	$ 640	665	$ 950	2,150	5,555	$10,800
1994	475	490	*545	600	*930	*2,330	6,000
Individual Pricing (1994)							
1937-P	$ 65	$ 70	$ 75	$ 90	$ 160	$ 400	1,700
1937-D	205	210	235	255	340	550	1,800
1937-S	205	210	235	255	375	700	2,500

Percent of mintage certified..17%, 25%, 22%
Popular collector grades...MS64-65 Popular investor grades....................................MS65-66
Background: 200th anniversary of Daniel Boone's birth

Comments

The 1937 Boone set is similar to the 1935/34 set. The P mint is common and the mintmarked issues have extremely low mintages (tied for 9th out of 144). As you would expect, the P mint trades as type in every grade. The D and S bring strong premiums over type, particularly in the lower grades. Due to the extremely low mintages, there are not enough circulated and low mint-state coins to satisfy collector demand. Dealers who usually sell AU50-MS60 raw coins are forced to purchase MS63 or 64 coins to fill their orders. Because of this, there is not much difference in price between MS60 and MS64 grades. The D and S have similar rarities up to grade 65 with the S being just a bit tougher. The S will command a small premium in 64 and a moderate premium in 65 versus the D. In grades above 65 the S is harder to locate. The surprisingly close population in 66 between the D and S is deceiving. S mint coins are quite a bit tougher and always command a moderate/substantially higher premium. Part of the explanation lies in an unusually high NGC pop for this coin (see Appendix *Table A-2*).

All 3 coins from this issue come nice but look different. The '37-P is similar to the earlier common issues. The D comes frosty with a hard luster and the S is similar, with tendencies toward proof-like fields and a relatively high proof-like population. The low mintage aspect of this set combined with the relatively low MS65 rankings of the D and S make it very attractive. 1937 Boones, particularly the mintmarked issues, sell quickly. This set is one of my favorites.

✓ Avoid paying more than type money for the '37-P. This is a common scam.
✓ Do not buy this issue in grades below certified MS64.
✓ Low mintage, high basal value issue that is likely to be hoarded.
✓ Author's choice: *Collector* MS64; *Investor* MS65. This issue is Highly Recommended.

TIPS!

Boone
1938-P, D, S

Mintage
Business strikes: 2100, 2100, 2100
Ranking: (3)   (3)   (3)

Certified Populations & Historical Values

	MS60	MS62	MS63	MS64	MS65	MS66	MS67
38-P: Pop	0	10	60	207	210	43	5
Rank	(1)	(31)	(18)	(11)	(32)	(47)	(57)
38-D: Pop	0	10	52	193	204	89	19
Rank	(1)	(31)	(17)	(8)	(31)	(66)	(91)
38-S: Pop	0	17	76	179	169	60	19
Rank	(1)	(53)	(29)	(4)	(23)	(53)	(91)
Set Pricing							
1957	—	—	$ 185	—	—	—	—
1970	—	—	240	—	—	—	—
1980	$1,250	—	1,500	—	$1,850	—	—
1982	775	—	975	—	1,500	$2,625	—
1989	925	$ 975	1,075	$1,450	3,075	6,200	$15,500
1994	660	705	780	885	1,685	*2735	8,100
Individual Pricing (1994)							
1938-P	$ 220	$ 235	$ 260	$ 295	$ 540	$ 950	$ 3,350
1938-D	220	235	260	295	540	750	2,500
1938-S	220	235	260	295	605	875	2,250

Percent of mintage certified..25%, 27%, 25%
Popular collector grades............................MS63-65 Popular investor grades..........................MS65-66
Background: 200th anniversary of Daniel Boone's birth

Comments

The 1938 set is the king of the Boones. Like the other multi-year sets, the last year of issue is the scarcest. Other members of this club would be the '39 Arks, '39 Oregons and '38 Texas. These sets have all proved popular with collectors because of their low mintages. These sets are hoarded and when nice coins are available they usually sell rapidly. Up to grade 64, the '38 Boones all have similar values and scarcities. In MS65 the difference in ranking that began in 64 becomes significant enough for the S mint to command a moderate premium. It should be noted that the population rankings in 64 and 65 are quite low for moderately priced coins.* In MS66 and MS67 the rarity scale changes and the P mint takes over as the toughest coin.

Differences in this grade range are usually accounted for by production quality (i.e. 1938-P's were not made as well as 1938-D's and S's). All three coins come nice and are generally available up to 65 in frosty white. Even some 66 coins are available white but often have some light toning or pretty rim color. Because of the consistent mintages, these coins are often encountered as sets. Matched pieces with attractive coloration will command small to moderate premiums particularly in grades 65 and 66. This set is also one of my favorites and I strongly recommend purchases in grades 64 and above. The S mint also comes proof-like.

*Note: Most PDS coins have more appealing cost versus pop ranking numbers than single-coin issues. You can interpret this two ways. Either the PDS coins are underrated or demand is less because they are not part of the 50-piece type set. I feel the truth is partly both these explanations. The PDS coins are underrated but not as much as it would seem.

✓ High basal value, purchase only MS64 and higher.
✓ Issue is subject to hoarding.
✓ Avoid coins that are washed out or have mottled toning.
✓ Author's choice: *Collector* MS64; *Investor* MS65. This issue is Highly Recommended.

TIPS!

Harry Laibstain

Bridgeport
1936

Mintage
Business strikes: 25,015
Ranking: (100)

Certified Populations & Historical Values

	MS60	MS62	MS63	MS64	MS65	MS66	MS67
Pop.	7	111	623	1,794	1,169	214	10
Rank	(114)	(112)	(121)	(136)	(130)	(103)	(72)
Pricing							
1957	—	—	$ 10	—	—	—	—
1970	—	—	26	—	—	—	—
1980	$ 140	—	200	—	$ 350	—	—
1982	105	—	145	—	220	$ 440	—
1989	130	$ 140	150	$ 375	1,475	5,800	$9,050
1994	85	90	95	130	380	1,100	5,100

Percent of mintage certified..16%
Popular collector grades..............................MS63-64   Popular investor grades.................................MS65-66
Background: 100th anniversary of the incorporation of Bridgeport, Connecticut

Comments

The Bridgeport commemorative is one of many issues from the late 1930's. In general, coins from this time frame were well preserved by collectors. From grade MS62 to 66, Bridgeports have fairly consistent population rankings. This issue should be considered common with some condition rarity developing on the top end (MS66 and MS67).

The Bridgeport has some quality problems due to the design. In addition to open fields, the devices both obverse and reverse are flat and exposed. Marks, scrapes and hairlines are picked up and show easily. Remarkably, many gem quality 65 coins exist and its ranking is near the bottom of the series. The ranking improves somewhat in 66 but not enough, when coupled with the coin's lack of popularity, to justify its current 66 price. Investors should note significant drops since 1989 in grades 64 and 65. At today's levels, these grades are probably fairly priced. Bridgeports can be found up to MS65 with frosty white luster or very light toning. Expect a few ticks or some light hairlines even in the higher grades. MS66 coins should be gems without any significant defects.

✓ Be fussy when purchasing this issue in grades above 65. Expect a few ticks on MS65 coins.
✓ Look for subtle hairlines on the reverse eagle.
✓ Coins with real eye appeal from this issue are rare and will command a moderate to substantial premium.
✓ Author's choice: *Collector* MS64; *Investor* MS65.

California
1925-S

Mintage
Business strikes: 86,394
Ranking: (122)

Certified Populations & Historical Values

	MS60	MS62	MS63	MS64	MS65	MS66	MS67
Pop.	25	404	997	1,162	661	269	45
Rank	(136)	(137)	(133)	(113)	(93)	(113)	(118)
Pricing							
1957	—	—	$ 12	—	—	—	—
1970	—	—	20	—	—	—	—
1980	$ 150	—	275	—	$ 650	—	—
1982	90	—	140	—	255	$ 510	—
1989	120	$ 185	310	$ 525	2,450	5,400	$ 8,125
1994	75	115	190	290	725	1,400	4,000

Percent of mintage certified..4%
Popular collector grades.................................MS62-64   Popular investor grades.................................MS65-67
Background: 75th anniversary of California in the Union

Comments

This high-mintage, high-population issue is much tougher than its numbers indicate. Because of the state of California's size and large collector base, these coins experience strong regional demand. In addition, the California is widely regarded as one of the most attractive commemorative designs. These coins were well made and come with a bright reflective luster. White coins are highly sought after and available in all grades up to MS67. A few years ago several gem brilliant rolls came onto the market via a California dealer. I was fortunate enough to buy nearly a roll of slabbed 65 and 66 coins that were just incredible. Some of these went on to higher grades.

MS63 and MS64 coins that are white sell almost immediately. As a dealer I never have enough in inventory. Higher grades also sell well as this coin is also popular among investors. Increased populations since 1989 partially offset the attractiveness of large price declines in grades MS65 to MS67. Although the mintage is not low, this issue is subject to hoarding. Prices of Californias in grades up to 64 are well supported by collectors. MS65 and 66 prices are supported by a combination of collector and investor demand. Purchases of MS67 coins should be considered speculative.

- ✓ Avoid spotty or dark-toned coins or coins with excessive water spots.
- ✓ Coins with attractive colors are available, expect to pay a premium.
- ✓ Tremendous demand function makes coin rarer than it appears.
- ✓ Author's choice: *Collector* MS64; *Investor* MS65. This issue is **Highly Recommended**.

Harry Laibstain

Cincinnati
1936-P, D, S

Mintage
Business strikes: 5005, 5005, 5006
Ranking: (22) (22) (27)

Certified Populations & Historical Values

	MS60	MS62	MS63	MS64	MS65	MS66	MS67
36-P: Pop	2	39	235	506	238	27	0
Rank	(93)	(89)	(84)	(74)	(37)	(32)	(1)
36-D: Pop	0	31	186	578	473	120	11
Rank	(1)	(78)	(76)	(85)	(71)	(75)	(74)
36-S: Pop	1	57	280	555	138	4	0
Rank	(66)	(100)	(91)	(80)	(14)	(4)	(1)
Set Pricing							
1957	—	—	$ 80	—	—	—	—
1970	—	—	330	—	—	—	—
1980	$1,300	—	1,650	—	$2,350	—	—
1982	600	—	850	—	1,250	$ 2,200	—
1989	820	$ 925	1,050	$1,600	8,275	33,000	$50,500
1994	630	660	705	840	2,200	*8250	25,500
Individual Pricing (1994)							
1936-P	$ 210	$ 220	$ 235	$ 275	$ 625	$ 2,400	—
1936-D	210	220	235	275	575	2,000	—
1936-S	210	220	235	290	1,000	2,800	—

Percent of mintage certified..21%, 28%, 21%
Popular collector grades............................MS63-65   Popular investor grades..................................MS65-67
Background: 50th anniversary of Cincinnati, Ohio as a music center

Comments

This moderately low-mintage, single-year PDS set is popular both as a type coin and in sets. All three coins trade as type up to grade 64 with only the S carrying a small premium (in 64) and then only if its nice. In MS65 the rarity of all 3 coins is considerably different as you can see by their rankings of 37, 71 and 14 respectively. The D is obviously the best quality and can be found with a thick fresh luster. The P can also be found white in MS65 but the quality is usually a notch below the D mint. The S mint coin is almost never found nice and most 65 examples I have encountered are either average or below. Finding a nice S mint or even an untoned specimen is almost impossible above 64. This set often comes with toning and attractively toned multi-colored coins do command a premium. The design of this coin lends itself to several quality problems. The fields are wide open on both sides and the coin has a high relief. Areas prone to damage are Stephen Foster's cheek and jawbone (obverse) and the harp player's thighs (reverse).

Cincinnatis have a high basal value and prices in grades up to 64 are related. In 65 Cincinnatis become scarcer and take their first real jump in price. An even larger jump is registered in 66. MS65 coins seem appropriately priced and represent good value for the investor or advanced collector. MS66 coins may be a bit overpriced at present. Coins graded 67 are thinly traded and current prices may be misleading.

✓ Avoid dark, splotchy or stainy toning or heavy bag-marked coins that are common on this issue.
✓ AU/BU coins trade at only a small discount to MS63. Do not buy below this grade.
✓ Nice S mints in 64 and 65 command moderate and strong premiums.
✓ Author's choice: *Collector* <u>MS64</u>; *Investor* <u>MS65</u>. This issue is <u>Highly</u> <u>Recommended</u>.

Cleveland
1936

Mintage
Business strikes: 50,030
Ranking: (114)

Certified Populations & Historical Values

	MS60	MS62	MS63	MS64	MS65	MS66	MS67
Pop.	19	316	1,356	2,574	1,365	252	20
Rank	(128)	(132)	(141)	(142)	(135)	(109)	(94)
Pricing							
1957	—	—	$ 5	—	—	—	—
1970	—	—	15	—	—	—	—
1980	$ 70	—	100	—	$ 145	—	—
1982	50	—	75	—	130	$ 260	—
1989	85	$ 95	110	$ 250	1,675	4,995	$ 8,000
1994	50	52	55	85	235	1,275	4,500

Percent of mintage certified..................12%
Popular collector grades.............MS63-65 Popular investor grades.............MS65-67
Background: Centennial celebration of Cleveland. Issued during Great Lakes Expo of 1936

Comments

This high mintage issue ranks as one of the most common coins in the series. In grades 63-65 it finds itself among the bottom 4 of the 144-piece series. Although common, the Cleveland is popular because of its low price and geographical representation. Nice MS64 coins can currently be purchased for less than $100. MS65 and 66 prices are way off from their highs in 1989 but I do not believe this coin has strong investment potential due to its high populations and availability.

The Cleveland is generally available untoned in grades up to 65. The color is often just a shade off from white and the coin sometimes has a steely appearance. The coins occasionally come with multicolored toning and, as such, command a premium. Although not usually seen with heavy bag marks these coins often appear scuffy or lackluster. Current prices in grades up to 65 appear appropriate. At over five times the MS65 price, 66 coins appear overrated at present.

- ✓ Unlikely to ever be a rare coin.
- ✓ High mintage with a low percent certified may indicate increasing supply.
- ✓ Avoid dull-lustered coins.
- ✓ Author's choice: *Collector* MS64; *Investor* MS65.

Harry Laibstain

Columbian
1892

Mintage
Business strikes: 950,000
Ranking: (140)

Certified Populations & Historical Values

	MS60	MS62	MS63	MS64	MS65	MS66	MS67
Pop.	87	1,069	1,831	1,761	604	81	6
Rank	(142)	(143)	(143)	(135)	(87)	(62)	(62)
Pricing							
1957	—	—	$ 4	—	—	—	—
1970	—	—	5	—	—	—	—
1980	$ 22	—	50	—	$ 110	—	—
1982	19	—	42	—	150	$ 300	—
1989	55	$ 140	400	$1,200	4,800	10,100	$16,500
1994	30	40	90	215	535	2,175	13,500

Percent of mintage certified..1%
Popular collector grades.................................MS62-64   Popular investor grades...................................MS64-66
Background: Commemorate 400th anniversary of Columbus' discovery. Sold at the World's Fair in Chicago, 1893

Comments

The 1892 Columbian Expo half dollar was the first commemorative half dollar. Due to its high mintage, the 1892 is relatively available up to MS64. In grades 65 it becomes a little scarcer. There are two reasons for this: First, due to the design (especially the obverse) many specimens come with marks or friction in the cheek area. The relief is high enough on the obverse that when coins were stacked in rolls they abraded each other. In addition, the issue was not a sellout and many pieces were put into circulation. Although quite a few were rescued, at some level of mint state, not many true gems survived. The low percent certified (1%) shows that thousands of circulated Columbians exist today and will probably never be certified.

Columbians can be found up to grade 65 untoned with 63 and 64 coins being easier to locate in this state. Many coins come toned and some are quite dark and unappealing. In grades 65 and up it is not as easy as the rarity would indicate to find white or attractively toned specimens.

Do not be misled by the dramatic decreases in prices since 1989. This coin and its sister, the 1893, were run up in a large-scale promotion where investors were convinced Columbians would take off on the 500th anniversary of Columbus' discovery. This promotion left many investors "buried" in a relatively common coin that is currently priced about right in grades up to 65. MS66 specimens are probably overpriced at four times the cost of a 65.

✓ Can be found in proof-like and proofs exist.
✓ Avoid coins that are dark or have splotchy toning.
✓ Do not be misled by the majestic highs this coin once attained.
✓ Author's choice: *Collector* MS64; *Investor* MS65. This issue is Recommended.

Columbian
1893

Mintage
Business strikes: 1,550,405
Ranking: (143)

Certified Populations & Historical Values

	MS60	MS62	MS63	MS64	MS65	MS66	MS67
Pop.	116	1,229	1,772	1,522	396	42	1
Rank	(144)	(144)	(142)	(127)	(61)	(45)	(27)
Pricing							
1957	—	—	$ 3	—	—	—	—
1970	—	—	4	—	—	—	—
1980	$ 20	—	40	—	$ 110	—	—
1982	18	—	40	—	150	$ 300	—
1989	55	$ 140	400	$1,250	5,950	11,500	$16,700
1994	30	38	85	225	675	2,400	9,000

Percent of mintage certified ....<1%
Popular collector grades...MS62-65   Popular investor grades...MS65-66
Background: Commemorate 400th anniversary of Columbus' discovery. Sold at the World's Fair in Chicago, 1893

Comments

The 1893 Columbian has a mintage (50% greater than the 1892) and many were placed in circulation. In grades up to 64 this coin is ultra common, earning the title "most common commemorative in grades 60-63". Some rarity begins to develop in 64 and continues in earnest in grades 65 and above. The 1893 Columbian is actually rarer, in 65 and above, than the 1892 despite the over half million additional pieces minted.

1893's often exhibit a softer strike and weaker luster than the '92's. This coin is available in white or lightly toned examples up to grade 64. MS65's in white are rather scarce and will command a premium. The two areas most likely to show problems are Columbus' cheek and the sails on the reverse. Many cleaned and retoned examples of this issue exist. Prices for 63 to 65 graded coins are accurate for sight buyers, especially considering that many unappealing specimens would not be acceptable. MS66 examples, although considerably rarer than 1892's, seem pricey.

TIPS!
- ✓ Proofs and proof-likes do exist, though proof-likes are scarcer in this issue than the 1892.
- ✓ Avoid dark coins in any grade. This issue is plagued by them.
- ✓ Involved in the same promotion as 1892 Columbian; prices between 1989 and 1992 vastly overrated this coin's actual value.
- ✓ Author's choice: *Collector* MS64; *Investor* MS65. This issue is Recommended.

Harry Laibstain

Columbia
1936-P, D, S

Mintage
Business strikes: 9007, 8009, 8007
Ranking: (62) (60) (59)

Certified Populations & Historical Values

	MS60	MS62	MS63	MS64	MS65	MS66	MS67
36-P: Pop	0	22	144	577	777	320	33
Rank	(1)	(69)	(66)	(84)	(109)	(119)	(112)
36-D: Pop	0	15	132	402	668	507	112
Rank	(1)	(45)	(60)	(58)	(94)	(133)	(135)
36-S: Pop	0	17	154	458	696	475	51
Rank	(1)	(53)	(72)	(66)	(102)	(131)	(122)
Set Pricing							
1957	—	—	$ 48	—	—	—	—
1970	—	—	130	—	—	—	—
1980	$ 900	—	1,150	—	$1,850	—	—
1982	500	—	675	—	950	$1,900	—
1989	750	$ 825	870	$1,050	2,400	5,600	$13,200
1994	480	510	540	570	690	1,200	4,800
Individual Pricing (1994)							
1936-P	$ 160	$ 170	$ 180	$ 190	$ 230	$ 440	1,750
1936-D	160	170	180	190	230	380	1,450
1936-S	160	170	180	190	230	380	1,600

Percent of mintage certified...21%, 23%, 23%
Popular collector grades.............................MS65-66 Popular investor grades...................................MS65-67
Background: 150th Anniversary of the founding of Columbia, South Carolina

Comments

The Columbia, S.C., issues have relatively high mintages for a PDS set ranking 59th to 62nd in the series. The coins come clean with a frosty thick luster. These two factors insure a large supply of high quality coins, which is evident by the drop in rankings of MS65 and higher coins. With a population peak in grade 65 leaning toward 66, the Columbias are one of the highest quality issues in the entire series. Untoned coins in 66 are quite common and I have owned white MS67 coins. These coins are also available with nice toning but rarely command a large premium unless they are exceptional.

Columbias do enjoy some regional popularity but with a ready supply of high-grade coins, I believe current low pricing to be appropriate in grades up to 66. MS67 coins seem pricey at four times MS66 specimens. If you really like this issue, buy a nice set of 66's instead of one 67. As with many of the PDS sets, the D mint is the highest quality issue. If you're looking for incredible quality, the Denver issue may fill your order.

✓ Avoid dull or splotchy toned coins.
✓ Avoid any heavy bag marks in the open fields.
✓ Do not purchase this coin below grade 64.
✓ Author's choice: *Collector* MS65; *Investor* MS66.

Connecticut
1935

Mintage
Business strikes: 25,018
Ranking: (105)

Certified Populations & Historical Values

	MS60	MS62	MS63	MS64	MS65	MS66	MS67
Pop.	12	158	751	1,427	1,007	222	17
Rank	(122)	(118)	(128)	(123)	(125)	(104)	(89)
Pricing							
1957	—	—	$ 28	—	—	—	—
1970	—	—	41	—	—	—	—
1980	$ 220	—	285	—	$ 535	—	—
1982	185	—	245	—	400	$ 800	—
1989	210	$ 240	280	$ 525	2,100	4,450	$ 7,550
1994	150	170	175	270	500	1,710	4,520

Percent of mintage certified............14%
Popular collector grades...........MS63-64   Popular investor grades............MS65-67
Background: 300th anniversary of the founding of the colony of Connecticut

Comments

The Connecticut half dollar, with its relatively high mintage, has a consistent ranking throughout the grade range. In every grade except 67 this coin ranks above 100. Although not rare, it is difficult to locate nice examples of the Connecticut in any grade. The coin suffers from several problems, most notably scuffiness and/or hairlining on the high points and splotchy or dull surfaces. When available with pure white frosty surfaces, this coin is very attractive and the luster will have a ring to it. These examples are my favorites and sell quickly. Many beautifully toned specimens exist, and when available, they command a moderate premium. I feel this coin is currently priced about right and nice examples do have potential, despite moderately high populations.

✓ Watch for hidden problems on the bird's wing area.
✓ Avoid coins with spots or unappealing toning.
✓ High basal value, do not purchase below grade 63.
✓ Author's choice: *Collector* MS64; *Investor* MS65. This issue is Recommended.

TIPS!

Harry Laibstain

Delaware
1936

Mintage
Business strikes: 20,993
Ranking: (98)

Certified Populations & Historical Values

	MS60	MS62	MS63	MS64	MS65	MS66	MS67
Pop.	5	121	536	1,402	1,072	295	19
Rank	(112)	(114)	(118)	(122)	(127)	(116)	(91)
Pricing							
1957	—	—	$ 14	—	—	—	—
1970	—	—	38	—	—	—	—
1980	$ 220	—	285	—	$ 535	—	—
1982	165	—	200	—	300	$ 600	—
1989	225	$ 250	270	$ 500	1,900	5,300	$ 8,400
1994	160	188	190	230	550	1,130	4,040

Percent of mintage certified...16%
Popular collector grades...................................MS63-65   Popular investor grades...................................MS65-67
Background: 300th anniversary of the landing of the Swedish colonists in Delaware

Comments

The Delaware commemorative has a moderate mintage and fairly high population rankings in all grades, similar to the Connecticut. These single-issue coins may seem rather common when viewed in the context of the 144 piece-set which contains many PDS sets and multiple-year issues. Although any single Texas except the '34 has a significantly lower mintage, coins like Delaware and Connecticut will always trade at higher levels and have as good, if not better, investment potential because of their overall demand as a single-issue type coin (see *Tables 6 & 8*).

The Delaware design lends itself to several problems. The roof of the church and surrounding open field areas, as well as the ships sails on the reverse, are prone to scuffs and hairlines. In addition, it's not unusual to see splotchy, unappealing toning on this issue. For these reasons, attractive mark-free specimens that are white or lightly toned sell quickly and usually at moderate to strong premiums. Like so many commemoratives, this coin has a strong basal value and should not be purchased below grade 63 or 64. At current prices, these grades represent good value for collectors. MS65 and MS66 specimens are reasonably priced in relation to current rarity and demand.

✓ Proof-likes exist but show little contrast.
✓ Don't be afraid to pay premiums for cosmetic coins with nice luster.
✓ Mintage and population underrate the coins true availability.
✓ Author's choice: *Collector* MS64; *Investor* MS65. This issue is Highly Recommended.

Elgin
1936

Mintage
Business strikes: 20,015
Ranking: (96)

Certified Populations & Historical Values

	MS60	MS62	MS63	MS64	MS65	MS66	MS67
Pop.	0	50	489	1,806	1,734	461	57
Rank	(1)	(94)	(114)	(137)	(138)	(130)	(125)
Pricing							
1957	—	—	$ 15	—	—	—	—
1970	—	—	33	—	—	—	—
1980	$ 190	—	275	—	$ 460	—	—
1982	140	—	175	—	250	$ 500	—
1989	250	$ 260	270	$ 450	1,600	4,500	$ 8,000
1994	170	175	180	195	260	780	3,300

Percent of mintage certified..23%
Popular collector grades...MS64-65   Popular investor grades...MS65-67
Background: 100th anniversary of the founding of Elgin, Illinois

Comments

Although the Elgin has a moderate mintage ranking for a single issue, the coin is not underrated. Unlike the Connecticut and Delaware on the preceding pages, the Elgin comes nice with a thick, strong, frosty luster. This is evidenced by the high populations and rankings in grades 66 and 67. The only quality problems this coin suffers is from light bag marks or weak strikes. In choice BU its intense luster makes it a beautiful coin. Coins with attractive toning are available and command moderate premiums.

Do not be misled by 1989 prices on this issue. High populations almost guarantee that those levels will not be repeated in the future. Current levels are about right and downside has all but been eliminated. MS66 and MS67 specimens may be the only exception to this statement. Insist on a high quality example for your collection; they should be available.

✓ Avoid poorly struck coins.
✓ Purchase coins with thick frosty luster and minimal marks.
✓ Do not buy this issue below grade 64.
✓ Author's choice: *Collector* MS65; *Investor* MS65.

Harry Laibstain

Gettysburg
1936

Mintage
Business strikes: 26,928
Ranking: (107)

Certified Populations & Historical Values

	MS60	MS62	MS63	MS64	MS65	MS66	MS67
Pop.	0	120	660	1,633	1,077	231	31
Rank	(1)	(113)	(123)	(132)	(128)	(107)	(110)
Pricing							
1957	—	—	$ 15	—	—	—	—
1970	—	—	36	—	—	—	—
1980	$ 275	—	400	—	$ 700	—	—
1982	190	—	230	—	350	$ 700	—
1989	225	$ 265	305	$ 525	2,075	6,250	$14,000
1994	185	195	215	280	550	1,540	3,600

Percent of mintage certified..14%
Popular collector grades..........................MS62-64 Popular investor grades..................................MS65-67
Background: 75th anniversary of the Civil War Battle of Gettysburg, Pennsylvania

Comments

The Gettysburg is a very popular Civil War issue. It is often collected in a 4-piece set with the Antietam, Grant and the Lincoln. The design, although busy, is considered attractive and intricate. The obverse is prone to marks and scuffs on the faces of the veterans and on the reverse flags. Finding clean, mark-free coins is difficult. Expect some light hairlining or even a few small ticks in these areas up to grade 65. Beyond that, any imperfections should be very slight. Gettysburgs are available in white up to 64. In 65 some white coins are available but, more often, light original toned examples are offered.

Gettysburgs have always been easy to sell and I buy all appealing examples I can up to 65. The coin becomes expensive in 66 and this premium may not be justified in light of the 231 coins certified. Even so, it is more reasonably priced than many similar 66 issues and is not far from being appropriately priced. A moderate correction in price would make this coin appealing. This issue is hoarded, particularly in grades up to 65. Don't let the high ranking scare you away from purchasing this issue. Remember, supply is only one part of the equation and demand for this coin is strong.

✓ High basal value, only buy grades 63 and above.
✓ Avoid coins with heavy cuts that plague this issue.
✓ Attractively toned examples are available and command a moderate premium.
✓ Author's choice: *Collector* MS64; *Investor* MS65. This issue is Highly Recommended.

Grant
1922

Mintage
Business strikes: 67,405
Ranking: (117)

Certified Populations & Historical Values

	MS60	MS62	MS63	MS64	MS65	MS66	MS67
Pop.	21	332	1,017	1,180	546	89	12
Rank	(133)	(134)	(134)	(115)	(82)	(66)	(79)
Pricing							
1957	—	—	$ 11	—	—	—	—
1970	—	—	21	—	—	—	—
1980	$ 95	—	150	—	$ 325	—	—
1982	75	—	120	—	320	$ 640	—
1989	90	$ 150	325	$ 775	4,100	7,700	$16,500
1994	65	95	180	300	805	2,100	9,000

Percent of mintage certified...5%
Popular collector grades....................................MS62-64   Popular investor grades.................................MS65-66
Background: The 100th anniversary of the birth of Ulysses S. Grant

Comments

The Grant is popular because of its Civil War connection and the availability of high-quality specimens. As you might expect, the high mintage makes this coin relatively common in grades up through MS64. Grants are available with frosty white luster through grades MS66. Untoned MS63 and 64 coins sell quickly. These coins are often difficult to distinguish from higher grades and many of these sell for PQ prices. Grants get progressively harder to locate as the grade increases. MS65 and MS66 examples, while not rare, seem to enjoy steady demand. MS65 coins with decent eye appeal sell fast relative to other 65 commems with similar rarity and pricing structures.

Due to the busy design, the reverse always appears nice. Watch for problems on the obverse in Grants forehead and hair. It is not unusual to see Grants with die polishing in the obverse fields. This does not affect desirability unless they are excessive or there are additional hairlining problems. In grades 65 and below, current pricing on the Grants seems about right. Coins MS66 and above are pricey and a bit speculative.

- ✓ Avoid mottled, toned coins that are plentiful in this issue.
- ✓ Nice NGC Grants may be a bargain as they often trade at substantial discounts to PCGS coins.
- ✓ This is a high demand issue.
- ✓ Author's choice: *Collector* MS64; *Investor* MS65. This issue is Recommended.

Harry Laibstain

Grant/Star
1922

Mintage
Business strikes: 4,256
Ranking: (20)

Certified Populations & Historical Values

	MS60	MS62	MS63	MS64	MS65	MS66	MS67
Pop.	13	148	322	296	90	14	1
Rank	(123)	(116)	(96)	(31)	(3)	(17)	(27)
Pricing							
1957	—	—	$ 100	—	—	—	—
1970	—	—	90	—	—	—	—
1980	$ 700	—	1,100	—	$ 2,300	—	—
1982	500	—	900	—	5,000	$ 7,500	—
1989	560	$ 880	2,350	$ 6,850	21,750	39,000	$67,500
1994	730	1,200	1,460	2,600	7,000	17,000	40,000

Percent of mintage certified..21%
Popular collector grades...MS60-64 Popular investor grades.................................MS64-66
Background: The 100th anniversary of the birth of Ulysses S. Grant

Comments

The Grant/Star is identical to the Grant except for an incuse star in right obverse field. Due to its low mintage (lowest of any commemorative, excluding PDS singles – see *Table 1*), this issue is extremely popular and always in demand. Its relatively high ranking in lower grades is misleading. These coins are often hoarded and they sell quickly. In fact, the lower the grade, the quicker they sell — an effect related to affordability. Quality conscious collectors usually focus on 63 and 64 examples, which are popular in white or the light, original toning typical of this issue. High-end coins in these grades almost always sell for a premium. MS65 issues are rare as evidenced by its No. 3 ranking (excluding PDS issues it is the No. 1 ranked commem in 65 – see *Table 5*).

In MS66, the ranking moves down at least partially due to a discrepancy in the way PCGS and NGC grade these coins. Of the 14 pieces graded 66, twelve come from the NGC population. Since PCGS 66 coins are scarcer, they carry a stiff premium over their NGC 66 counterparts. It is unlikely that any of these 12 would grade 66 at PCGS; due to the large difference in value, most have undoubtedly been tried for crossover. To a lesser extent the same situation exists in the 64 and 65 populations even though pricing differences between the grading services are smaller. In grades below 64 the relationship of coins graded by PCGS and NGC is more in line and price differences between the services are smaller, if at all.

Prices for coins graded 63 and lower are very firm and well supported by collectors. MS64 coins are also solid at current levels and are pursued by investors and advanced collectors. MS65 coins are generally unavailable and the coins I have had sold immediately. The market for MS66 and 67 coins is thin. Shop prices before purchasing one of these gems.

✓ Often hoarded by collectors and investors.
✓ High-grade NGC coins should sell at a discount to PCGS coins.
✓ Look out for cleaned and reworked coins.
✓ Author's choice: *Collector* MS63; *Investor* MS65. This issue is Highly Recommended.

TIPS!

Hawaiian
1921

Mintage
Business strikes: 9,958
Ranking: (69)

Certified Populations & Historical Values

	MS60	MS62	MS63	MS64	MS65	MS66	MS67
Pop.	20	225	466	623	203	25	0
Rank	(130)	(128)	(110)	(91)	(30)	(30)	(1)
Pricing							
1957	—	—	$ 125	—	—	—	—
1970	—	—	425	—	—	—	—
1980	$ 1,400	—	1,850	—	$ 3,000	—	—
1982	600	—	800	—	1,350	$ 2,350	—
1989	700	$ 1,050	1,650	$ 4,575	15,600	27,100	$36,000
1994	845	1,125	1,430	1,960	4,160	11,000	20,000

Percent of mintage certified..16%
Popular collector grades...............................MS60-64   Popular investor grades.................................MS64-66
Background: 150th anniversary of Captain Cook's arrival on the Hawaiian Islands

Comments

The Hawaiian is one of the most popular and attractive coins in the series. Even though it ranks 69th in mintage, the number made is still considered very low. If you take out the PDS issues, it has the 4th lowest mintage in the series and, as a single-issue type coin, it has the lowest mintage of any commemorative. Don't be misled by the high population rankings in the lower grades. Like other scarce commems, Hawaiians have heavy population concentrations in lower grades and appear more available than they are. In addition, regrading also plays a role in the scarcer, more valuable coin's population statistics.

The Hawaiian has large open field areas on both sides and a tendency toward hairline problems. I have seen many attractive 62 or 63 coins that would grade higher if not for this. White coins are available in grades up to 65 but usually carry a premium. Many Hawaiians are toned in varying degrees. One large hoard that came out in the late 1980's from the Bank of Hawaii had a significant amount of toned coins. These are still recognizable today for their encrusted gold and green colors.

Hawaiians in 64 and above have come down quite a bit since the record highs of 1989. It is interesting to note that while the higher grades have declined, lower grades have risen. If prices push up from the bottom, MS63 and MS64 coins may move up next. These grades represent solid value and have strong possibilities for growth. In grades above 64, the Hawaiian is a scarce coin and the MS65 ranking of 30th equates to a ranking of 9th, excluding PDS issues. Prices for Hawaiians in grades 63 and below remain quite firm. MS64 coins are supported by both collectors and investors and is my favorite grade in this issue. MS65 coins are in heavy demand by investors and, although they take a large jump in price, appear to be appropriately priced.

✓ Available with pretty multicolored toning.
✓ High basal value; recommended minimum grade to purchase is MS62.
✓ Good growth potential on this hoarded issue.
✓ Author's choice: *Collector* MS64; *Investor* MS65. This issue is Highly Recommended.

Harry Laibstain

Hudson
1935

Mintage
Business strikes: 10,008
Ranking: (76)

Certified Populations & Historical Values

	MS60	MS62	MS63	MS64	MS65	MS66	MS67
Pop.	13	158	647	932	434	68	3
Rank	(123)	(118)	(122)	(102)	(65)	(56)	(47)
Pricing							
1957	—	—	$ 80	—	—	—	—
1970	—	—	210	—	—	—	—
1980	$ 700	—	950	—	$ 1,350	—	—
1982	400	—	575	—	950	$ 1,900	—
1989	450	$ 525	675	$ 1,925	5,900	11,450	$19,000
1994	380	420	450	600	1,330	3,100	11,000

Percent of mintage certified..23%
Popular collector grades...........................MS62-64   Popular investor grades................................MS65-66
Background: 150th anniversary of Hudson, New York

Comments

The Hudson is another-low mintage issue (tied for 5th excluding PDS sets and 2nd as a single-issue type coin). Like the Hawaiian and Grant/Star, the certified population tends to be concentrated in the lower grades and the rankings are misleading. The MS65 ranking of 65th is equivalent to 13th when PDS issues are subtracted. The Hudson is a scarce coin in all grades. Investors should note the large price declines in grades 64-66 since 1989.

The design of this coin leads to some quality problems. The obverse (considered by the grading services to be the dated side of the coin) is prone to marks and hairlines, particularly in the center field and around King Neptune. On the reverse, the ship's sails pick up scuffs and lines. The center sail is almost always flatly struck. This coin also suffers some coloration problems, and mottled or unappealing toning is not uncommon. Nice looking coins in any grade are desirable; be prepared to pay a premium for these. This is a popular coin with an interesting design from a high population state. Current values seem low particularly on grades 63-65. The current market supply is thin and nice examples are the exception. Also collected as part of a sub-set of commems bearing ship designs.

- ✓ Underrated issue. Prices in 63 and 64 are very low.
- ✓ Avoid coins with negative eye appeal.
- ✓ High basal value, minimum recommended MS63.
- ✓ Author's choice: *Collector* MS64; *Investor* MS65. This issue is Highly Recommended.

Huguenot
1924

Mintage
Business strikes: 142,080
Ranking: (132)

Certified Populations & Historical Values

	MS60	MS62	MS63	MS64	MS65	MS66	MS67
Pop.	10	174	778	1,545	683	142	7
Rank	(121)	(124)	(129)	(131)	(100)	(83)	(65)
Pricing							
1957	—	—	$ 11	—	—	—	—
1970	—	—	21	—	—	—	—
1980	$ 95	—	175	—	$ 360	—	—
1982	80	—	120	—	275	$ 550	—
1989	90	$ 125	210	$ 800	3,500	6,200	$ 9,700
1994	57	65	80	160	600	1,490	6,500

Percent of mintage certified......2%
Popular collector grades......MS63-64   Popular investor grades......MS65-66
Background: 300th anniversary of the settling of the Huguenots and Walloons in the New World

Comments

The Huguenot has a high mintage and high population that keeps its price low in grades below MS64. Above 64, prices rise dramatically due to increasing scarcity. This is probably related to storage and handling of this early commem rather than production quality. The coin's design also plays a role in high-grade scarcity. Huguenots can come with blazing mint luster and often have a bright, chromelike finish. Die polish is not unusual. This issue is notorious for its little polished spot to the left of the upper left sail. Other problem areas are Admiral Coligny's cheekbone and the open fields on the reverse.

This coin is available white in grades up to 66. Nice examples, especially in the lower grades will command some premium. Huguenots, while not scarce, are in demand and sell well. Dramatic drops since 1989, especially in grades 64-65, make this coin attractive to the Investor. MS66 coins are fully priced.

✓ Popular collector coin / New York commem.
✓ Avoid stained or washed out specimens.
✓ Only 2% of mintage graded.
✓ Author's choice: *Collector* <u>MS64</u>; *Investor* <u>MS65</u>. This issue is <u>Highly</u> <u>Recommended</u>.

TIPS!

Harry Laibstain

Iowa
1946

Mintage
Business strikes: 100,057
Ranking: (126)

Certified Populations & Historical Values

	MS60	MS62	MS63	MS64	MS65	MS66	MS67
Pop.	3	84	514	1,836	3,335	1,782	278
Rank	(100)	(109)	(116)	(138)	(142)	(144)	(141)
Pricing							
1957	—	—	$ 8	—	—	—	—
1970	—	—	20	—	—	—	—
1980	$ 75	—	100	—	$ 175	—	—
1982	55	—	70	—	100	$ 200	—
1989	80	$ 90	105	$ 175	650	1,125	$ 2,400
1994	55	61	64	68	80	150	690

Percent of mintage certified..8%
Popular collector grades..................................MS64-66 Popular investor grades..................................MS65-68
Background: 100th anniversary of Iowa's statehood

Comments

The Iowa is one of the set's most common coins in high grade. Up to 64, the coin essentially trades at basal value. If there is any scarcity of Iowas, it's in these lower grades. In grades 65-67 Iowas rank 3rd, 1st and 4th from the bottom. Only the two San Diego commems are more common in 65. Nothing is more common in 66. In 67, Iowas are only slightly less common than the '37-D Oregon, York and Norfolk.

Nearly all Iowas were distributed in Iowa and many were sold in groups or mini hoards. With only 8% graded so far, a strong possibility exists that more Iowas will show up. Iowas are available in white up to MS67. Although I have seen some toned Iowas, they are the exception. Due to the busy design, they do not show marks easily. In addition, they come with a thick frosty luster. These factors contribute to making the Iowa a common high-quality commemorative with a moderately popular design.

Price drops have been significant over the last several years. Current levels make this coin look enticing, however investment growth will only come if sales promotions can take excess coins off the market and keep them off. Current prices seem like a bargain but are an accurate representation of value.

- ✓ Hoards exist; 25 and 50 coin lots are not unusual but have come out less frequently in recent years.
- ✓ Pop 13 in MS68 and 12 are PCGS.
- ✓ Minimum recommended grade to purchase, MS65.
- ✓ Author's choice: *Collector* MS65; *Investor* MS66.

Lexington
1925

Mintage
Business strikes: 162,013
Ranking: (134)

Certified Populations & Historical Values

	MS60	MS62	MS63	MS64	MS65	MS66	MS67
Pop.	24	309	1,118	1,540	477	54	1
Rank	(135)	(130)	(136)	(130)	(72)	(51)	(27)
Pricing							
1957	—	—	$ 8	—	—	—	—
1970	—	—	12	—	—	—	—
1980	$ 70	—	100	—	$ 150	—	—
1982	40	—	70	—	175	$ 350	—
1989	50	$ 70	130	$ 575	2,500	7,050	$12,200
1994	57	65	80	160	925	3,100	6,000

Percent of mintage certified..4%
Popular collector grades.................................MS63-64 Popular investor grades................................MS65-66
Background: 150th anniversary of the Revolutionary War battle of Lexington and Concord, Massachusetts

Comments

The high mintage of the Lexington insures a ready supply of lower-grade coins. Not until MS64 does the coin's price take a significant jump and this is related more to its value in 65 than its rarity in 64. Excluding PDS coins, the Lexington would rank 15th in MS65 (see *Table 7*). It is available white in grades up to 64. MS65's usually have a light patina but do occasionally come untoned. Expect to pay a premium for PQ 64 coins because of the large spread to 65.

The Lexington is difficult to get into a 65 holder because of its design. There is a tremendous amount of open area on both sides and the corner of the belfry is subject to friction and striking problems. In addition, the luster has a tendency to be more chrome-like in appearance than frosty. Lexingtons are popular and are often collected with the other battle commems, besides being part of the 50-piece type set.

Nice 63 and 64 coins sell quickly as their moderate prices make them desirable to collectors. MS65 coins also sell remarkably well considering the price jump. This is due primarily to investor purchases based on population rarity. Lexingtons above 65 are priced speculatively and should be purchased only by individuals who accept significant risk/reward ratios in their coin investing.

✓ High mintage is misleading regarding rarity in high grades.
✓ Avoid dark or mottled toned examples in this issue.
✓ Sometimes seen with the small wooden box, coins were originally sold with.
✓ Author's choice: *Collector* MS64; *Investor* MS65. This issue is Recommended.

Harry Laibstain

Lincoln
1918

Mintage
Business strikes: 100,058
Ranking: (129)

Certified Populations & Historical Values

	MS60	MS62	MS63	MS64	MS65	MS66	MS67
Pop.	15	315	1,200	1,698	773	168	31
Rank	(126)	(131)	(137)	(133)	(108)	(86)	(110)
Pricing							
1957	—	—	$ 11	—	—	—	—
1970	—	—	21	—	—	—	—
1980	$ 80	—	125	—	$ 225	—	—
1982	70	—	100	—	215	$ 430	—
1989	100	$ 130	160	$ 675	2,275	4,300	$ 6,025
1994	60	70	80	170	560	1,150	3,300

Percent of mintage certified..3%
Popular collector grades.................................MS63-64 Popular investor grades.................................MS65-67
Background: 100th anniversary of Illinois statehood

Comments

The Lincoln commemorative, like the Lexington, is common in grades to 64. Its high mintage insures a ready supply of low-grade and moderately priced coins. This issue takes a mild jump in price from 63 to 64 and a larger one to 65. With an MS65 ranking of 108, it is several hundred coins more common than the Lexington and thus is priced lower.

The coin suffers from some quality problems. Most notably, the obverse field in front of Lincoln's face is prone to scarring and hairlines. Luster quality is another trouble spot as it can range from gem frosty to dull and gray. Lustrous white coins do command a premium in this issue, especially in 64 and 65. In 65 many coins come with light toning or a mild russet patina. Lincolns seem to be priced about right and the coin's price relationships up through 66 seem appropriate. MS67 coins exist in quantity. Even at today's levels they seem expensive.

- ✓ Grade this coin mostly by the obverse.
- ✓ Low percentage of mintage certified.
- ✓ Don't be afraid to pay a moderate premium for PQ 64 and 65 examples.
- ✓ Author's choice: *Collector* MS64; *Investor* MS65. This issue is Recommended.

Long Island
1936

Mintage
Business strikes: 81,826
Ranking: (120)

Certified Populations & Historical Values

	MS60	MS62	MS63	MS64	MS65	MS66	MS67
Pop.	89	371	1,220	1,855	878	158	11
Rank	(143)	(136)	(137)	(133)	(108)	(86)	(110)
Pricing							
1957	—	—	$ 6	—	—	—	—
1970	—	—	14	—	—	—	—
1980	$ 65	—	85	—	$ 130	—	—
1982	50	—	64	—	105	$ 210	—
1989	80	$ 90	110	$ 375	2,425	5,700	$ 9,300
1994	50	53	55	100	340	1,550	4,500

Percent of mintage certified...6%
Popular collector grades...................................MS63-65 Popular investor grades.................................MS65-67
Background: 300th anniversary of the first European settlement on Long Island, New York

Comments

The Long Island has a high mintage and is plentiful in grades MS65 and below. Up to grade 63 all coins are worth about the same. From there on, the price begins to jump. Although ranked 108th in MS65, the relatively low price may leave some room for growth. I have seen this coin on several recommended lists over the last few years.

Long Islands are available white up to grades 64 and sometimes 65. MS65's usually have some light toning. Although the coin has virtually no open field areas, both sides are prone to bag marks and the ship's sails on the reverse are often hairlined, particularly on the center sail. Luster coloration is another problem area. White coins should be frosty white and lightly toned coins should have a subdued lustrous look with strong surface quality. Gem Long Islands often come with card toning from their original issue envelopes.

Although unlikely to appreciate in lower grades, price declines have been significant on this issue. Investors should note the 7 to 1 drops in MS65 since 1989. At nearly 5 times MS65 prices, 66 coins seem pricey. Investing in MS67 coins is speculative.

✓ Popular New York state issue.
✓ Only 6% of mintage certified, mini hoards could exist.
✓ Multicolor examples exist and generally command a premium.
✓ Author's choice: *Collector* MS64; *Investor* MS65. This issue is Recommended.

TIPS!

Harry Laibstain

Lynchburg
1936

Mintage
Business strikes: 20,013
Ranking: (94)

Certified Populations & Historical Values

	MS60	MS62	MS63	MS64	MS65	MS66	MS67
Pop.	2	76	478	1,241	1,104	361	53
Rank	(93)	(107)	(112)	(120)	(129)	(123)	(123)
Pricing							
1957	—	—	$ 15	—	—	—	—
1970	—	—	31	—	—	—	—
1980	$ 185	—	250	—	$ 450	—	—
1982	135	—	175	—	245	$ 490	—
1989	190	$ 200	220	$ 450	1,450	4,225	$ 6,800
1994	130	135	150	225	325	1,080	2,920

Percent of mintage certified..17%
Popular collector grades................................MS63-65   Popular investor grades................................MS65-67
Background: 150th anniversary of the charter to Lynchburg, Virginia

Comments

The certified populations of this issue have rather consistent rankings across the grade range. The mintage of 20,000 pieces might indicate a scarcer coin but, with 17% of these graded so far, it's relatively plentiful. The price increases gradually up to MS65.

Lynchburgs come frosty/creamy white and usually have nice surfaces. However, the coin does suffer a few quality problems. The obverse has some unprotected field areas and the coin is prone to scrapes and album lines across Carter Glass' face and forehead. Liberty's right leg and breast are subject to scrapes and cuts from stacking and inappropriate handling.

Lynchburg prices are very reasonable and the lower grades appear cheap. This coin suffers from lackluster demand because it's from a small city and the design is not particularly popular. At current levels, MS65 coins have some room for growth. MS66 and 67 coins seem pricey by comparison.

✓ Avoid coins with excessive cuts or scrapes in areas mentioned.
✓ Avoid dull and gray luster, these are available brilliant.
✓ Multicolored toned coins are available and trade for a premium. These were also issued in cards.
✓ Author's choice: *Collector* MS64; *Investor* MS65. This issue is Recommended.

Maine
1920

Mintage
Business strikes: 50,028
Ranking: (113)

Certified Populations & Historical Values

	MS60	MS62	MS63	MS64	MS65	MS66	MS67
Pop.	9	150	663	1,124	676	175	6
Rank	(118)	(117)	(124)	(112)	(97)	(90)	(62)
Pricing							
1957	—	—	$ 11	—	—	—	—
1970	—	—	21	—	—	—	—
1980	$ 100	—	175	—	$ 350	—	—
1982	85	—	160	—	390	$ 775	—
1989	90	$ 110	250	$ 600	2,850	7,500	$ 8,525
1994	65	85	135	260	610	1,710	8,500

Percent of mintage certified...6%
Popular collector grades...MS63-65 Popular investor grades...................................MS65-66
Background: The Centennial of Maine

Comments

The Maine commemorative has a relatively high mintage and is moderately common in grades to MS64 where the coin's population peaks. It is interesting to note that prices in MS62-64 approximately double with each notch in quality. These coins were sold for some years after their issue. Because of this and the low percent certified, hoards may exist.

The Maine is a moderately high-quality issue. The coin usually comes with good luster and white coins are readily available up to grade 65. However, some die polishing may be evident on the reverse which does not generally affect the grade. MS66 Maines usually have some color. Maines tend to pick up lines, especially on the obverse across the center of the coin and the two standing figures. The reverse has some open fields areas that are likely to pick up and show ticks and cuts easily.

Maines enjoy strong demand and appealing 63 and 64 grade coins sell quickly. MS65 coins also sell well at today's levels and may be a bit underpriced. Recently the market has come under pressure in this grade, as several mini-hoards of fresh white coins have come onto the market. At less than 1/4 of the 1989 high, MS65 coins appear cheap. MS66 coins are fully priced at today's level, and along with 67 coins, remain speculative as an investment.

- ✓ Avoid coins with unappealing toning or poor luster.
- ✓ Hoards may exist.
- ✓ Don't be afraid to pay a moderate premium for PQ coins in lower grades up to 65.
- ✓ Author's choice: *Collector* MS64; *Investor* MS65. This issue is Recommended.

Harry Laibstain

Maryland
1934

Mintage
Business strikes: 25,015
Ranking: (100)

Certified Populations & Historical Values

	MS60	MS62	MS63	MS64	MS65	MS66	MS67
Pop.	3	84	732	1,882	1,066	224	13
Rank	(100)	(109)	(127)	(140)	(126)	(106)	(81)
Pricing							
1957	—	—	$ 14	—	—	—	—
1970	—	—	31	—	—	—	—
1980	$ 160	—	200	—	$ 425	—	—
1982	105	—	150	—	330	$ 660	—
1989	135	$ 150	190	$ 550	1,725	4,900	$ 8,500
1994	110	120	130	160	330	1,130	5,500

Percent of mintage certified..16%
Popular collector grades.................................MS63-65 Popular investor grades.................................MS65-67
Background: 300th anniversary of the Maryland colony

Comments

The Maryland has a moderate mintage which, coincidentally, is exactly the same as the Bridgeport, Wisconsin and York. Due to a high demand by collectors, this issue has a strong basal value that influences the price through grade 64. The price then takes a jump in 65 as the population starts to drop off.

Marylands may come with brilliant luster or they may be subdued and have silver/gray surfaces. Many Marylands also come toned and it is not unusual to encounter dark or unappealing coins. Frosty white coins are actually rather scarce but, because of toning removers like Jewel Luster® there seems to be a ready supply of white Marylands. The fields on the obverse are open but do not pick up and show light ticks or hairlines easily. Marylands have textured surfaces that account for many of its characteristics. Lord Baltimore's face and hair usually have small depressions and cuts. Finding Marylands with clean obverse devices is not easy.

The prices of Marylands in grades to 63 have not changed much over the last 15 years and seem stable. MS64 and even MS65 coins, to a lesser extent, seem to be a bargain at current levels. MS66 coins are a bit pricey for their actual rarity. Most of these are toned and white MS66 coins are very scarce.

- ✓ Beware of washed out (dipped out) specimens.
- ✓ Avoid examples with deep cuts in the obverse fields.
- ✓ Original white coins or coins with pretty toning are most desirable in this issue.
- ✓ Author's choice: *Collector* MS64; *Investor* MS65. This issue is Recommended.

Missouri
1921

Mintage
Business strikes: 15,428
Ranking: (90)

Certified Populations & Historical Values

	MS60	MS62	MS63	MS64	MS65	MS66	MS67
Pop.	20	208	470	614	127	8	0
Rank	(130)	(127)	(111)	(90)	(12)	(11)	(1)
Pricing							
1957	—	—	$ 70	—	—	—	—
1970	—	—	112	—	—	—	—
1980	$ 775	—	1,150	—	$ 1,900	—	—
1982	365	—	625	—	1,350	$ 2,350	—
1989	325	$ 450	900	$ 4,300	17,000	26,100	$32,200
1994	265	380	555	910	5,600	15,500	19,000

Percent of mintage certified..10%
Popular collector grades...................................MS62-64 Popular investor grades MS64-66
Background: 100th anniversary of Missouri in the Union

Comments

Although the Missouri mintage is not particularly low, it is a tough coin to find and worth several hundred dollars in any mint state grade. Its mintage ranking of 90 is deceiving as it has the 9th lowest mintage in the series when PDS issues are excluded. The Missouri is available in lower grades but gets progressively harder to locate as the quality increases. This coin was very expensive in the late 1980's market and, while much lower now, is still one of the most valuable commemoratives in grades 64 and above.

One reason Missouris are scarce in high grades is because the surfaces, particularly the open obverse fields, often suffer from die polishing and hairlining. In addition, both sides have raised areas that get worn and show weak detail (on the obverse, the frontiersman's cheek and jaw; on the reverse, the frontiersman's legs, back and outstretched arm). Luster can be quite good on Missouris but this is often not the case. The Missouri is an early-issue commemorative (1921) and storage and handling were not as sophisticated then as in the mid to late '30's. Original, untoned specimens are scarce in any grade although nicely dipped white coins are available in grades up to 64. White 65 Missouris are really tough to locate and sell quickly when available.

Coins that grade 64 and below seem to be underpriced and current demand would probably support higher levels. MS65 coins, which have always seemed pricey to me, do not stay on the market long. When I consider how many collectors are building MS65 sets and then look at the populations, I realize why. Current values for MS65 coins are accurate because of low supply. Above grade 65 this issue is very expensive and not without significant risk.

✓ Nice examples, especially in grades 64 and below, should command a premium.
✓ Avoid mottled toning or coins with excessive scrapes on the high points.
✓ Investment potential in grades 63-65.
✓ Author's choice: *Collector* MS64; *Investor* MS65. This issue is Highly Recommended.

Harry Laibstain

Missouri 2★4
1921

Mintage
Business strikes: 5,000
Ranking: (21)

Certified Populations & Historical Values

	MS60	MS62	MS63	MS64	MS65	MS66	MS67
Pop.	8	172	423	525	100	3	0
Rank	(117)	(122)	(105)	(75)	(5)	(3)	(1)
Pricing							
1957	—	—	$ 72	—	—	—	—
1970	—	—	118	—	—	—	—
1980	$ 800	—	1,250	—	$ 2,100	—	—
1982	400	—	675	—	1,400	$ 2,450	—
1989	350	$ 515	1,125	$ 4,425	15,000	24,200	$31,300
1994	325	500	625	975	5,600	15,000	19,000

Percent of mintage certified...25%
Popular collector grades...................................MS62-64   Popular investor grades..................................MS64-65
Background: 100th anniversary of Missouri in the Union. 2x4 symbolizes 24th state

Comments

The Missouri 2x4 was struck before the plain Missouri and only 5000 coins were turned out, making it the second lowest mintage of any non-PDS coin. The population rankings between the two Missouris are quite similar in grades up to MS63 but some differences become apparent above this level. Even so, 2x4's in high grades carry little or no premium over the plain. They have very similar characteristics to the plains and suffer the same quality problems (see Missouri). There is a subtle difference in luster characteristics and strike, perhaps because these coins were struck first and in lower quantity. 2x4's tend to have slightly better luster and strike. This fact helps explain the similar certified populations among coins with such different mintages.

Another explanation is that 2x4's were purchased by more advanced collectors who stored and handled them better.

Missouri 2x4's trade at slightly higher prices than plains in grades up to 64. These coins are hoarded by many collectors and do not stay on the market long. Current demand for these grades could support higher prices. MS65 coins are expensive but the low supply and high demand seems to balance nicely at this level. Decent coins in MS65 also do not stay on the market long if priced right. MS65's are scarce in relation to demand and have good growth potential. Above 65, Missouris are very thinly traded and actual values are difficult to establish.

✓ Both Missouri issues are collected as type coins.
✓ Often hoarded because of low mintage.
✓ Light original toning, if not unattractive, should be acceptable and trades well in this issue.
✓ Author's choice: *Collector* MS64; *Investor* MS65. This issue is Highly Recommended.

Monroe
1923-S

Mintage
Business strikes: 274,077
Ranking: (136)

Certified Populations & Historical Values

	MS60	MS62	MS63	MS64	MS65	MS66	MS67
Pop.	34	461	1,086	999	196	38	5
Rank	(138)	(140)	(135)	(108)	(29)	(42)	(57)
Pricing							
1957	—	—	$ 8	—	—	—	—
1970	—	—	14	—	—	—	—
1980	$ 50	—	80	—	$ 175	—	—
1982	42	—	80	—	240	$ 480	—
1989	45	$ 60	250	$ 1,550	8,500	13,700	$17,600
1994	33	40	76	310	2,250	4,800	13,000

Percent of mintage certified...1%
Popular collector grades...................................MS63-64 Popular investor grades.................................MS64-66
Background: 100th anniversary of the Monroe Doctrine

Comments

The Monroe commemorative has an extremely high mintage which can be quite misleading when considering coins in high grade. It is extremely common in grades up to 63 and scarcer in grades 64 and above. In these higher grades, price levels have taken a real beating. MS64 coins are 1/5th of what they were in 1989 and MS65 and 66's have not fared much better. This issue has one of the lowest percentage of certified coins but don't expect any gem hoards to show up. Many Monroes have been mishandled and lightly circulated. They did not sell well and some were dumped into circulation. In addition, low-grade specimens are not worth much and are not usually sent in for certification.

Gem-quality Monroes are rare. The coin's luster is usually weak and its design rather flat. The open fields and flatness cause this coin to be easily frictioned. White coins are available up to grades 65 but above 63 they are scarce. High-grade examples usually have some toning and are not always appealing. Monroes are cheap in grades up to 62 and probably always will be. In grades 63 and 64, this issue is underrated and current demand could support higher prices for nice quality pieces. MS65 coins with their low population (ranking 29th, 8th without PDS issues) are very desirable. Because there are so many collector/investors for MS65 material, these coins remain pricey and generally unavailable. MS66 and 67 coins are speculative, with 66 prices being more realistic.

TIPS!

✓ Avoid coins with dull or spotty toning, which plagues this issue.
✓ Watch out for retoned or doctored coins.
✓ Majority of this issue is circulated or low grade mint state. Original gem coins are rare.
✓ Author's choice: *Collector* MS64; *Investor* MS65. This issue is Highly Recommended.

Harry Laibstain

New Rochelle
1938

Mintage
Business strikes: 15,266
Ranking: (89)

Certified Populations & Historical Values

	MS60	MS62	MS63	MS64	MS65	MS66	MS67
Pop.	0	30	259	1,192	1,340	363	47
Rank	(1)	(76)	(89)	(116)	(134)	(125)	(120)
Pricing							
1957	—	—	$ 25	—	—	—	—
1970	—	—	55	—	—	—	—
1980	$ 350	—	450	—	$ 825	—	—
1982	240	—	300	—	420	$ 840	—
1989	360	$ 380	400	$ 500	1,325	5,100	$ 7,650
1994	230	260	280	300	395	875	2,750

Percent of mintage certified...21%
Popular collector grades.............................MS64-65   Popular investor grades.................................MS65-67
Background: 250th Anniversary of New Rochelle, New York

Comments

The New Rochelle has a relatively low mintage for a non-PDS coin and has always been popular. As you can see from the chart, New Rochelles are much scarcer in low grades than in grades 64 and above. They usually have exceptional luster and minimal marks, surprising for a design with so much open area. If this issue were coined in the early '20's instead of the late '30's, it would probably not have remained the quality issue it is today. With a population peak in grade 65, the New Rochelle is one of the most common issues in gem condition, available untoned up to grade 66. It is not unusual for New Rochelles to have pretty toning and these pieces do command a premium. This coin is also available in varying degrees of proof-like surfaces and can be quite spectacular with reflective fields.

Up to grade 64, prices for New Rochelles reflect their high basal value. Many mail-order dealers do not really distinguish between a 62 and a 64. In 65, New Rochelles carry a moderate premium over basal value and are probably worth the difference. MS66 is the first grade where the coin experiences a real decline in supply and, therefore, the grade most investors focus on. MS67 coins are not easy to come by but they are available. Consider the price relationship of 66 to 67 before purchasing.

✓ Do not purchase this coin below grade 65.
✓ Purchase only coins with positive eye appeal.
✓ Low mintage belies this coin's actual rarity in high grades.
✓ Author's choice: *Collector* MS65; *Investor* MS66.

Norfolk
1936

Mintage
Business strikes: 16,936
Ranking: (91)

Certified Populations & Historical Values

	MS60	MS62	MS63	MS64	MS65	MS66	MS67
Pop.	0	27	153	526	1,237	1,415	423
Rank	(1)	(74)	(71)	(76)	(131)	(143)	(144)
Pricing							
1957	—	—	$ 20	—	—	—	—
1970	—	—	48	—	—	—	—
1980	$ 350	—	500	—	$ 825	—	—
1982	230	—	300	—	435	$ 870	—
1989	530	$ 540	550	$ 600	750	1,525	$ 2,300
1994	350	355	360	370	390	465	850

Percent of mintage certified..23%
Popular collector grades..MS64-66 Popular investor grades...MS66-68
Background: The 300th anniversary of Norfolk, Virginia

Comments

The Norfolk commem is the highest quality issue in the entire commemorative series, judging from its high certified populations in MS66 and above. Like the New Rochelle, it has a relatively low mintage but grades extremely high. Where the New Rochelle's population peaks in 65, the Norfolk peaks in 66, with a whopping 1,415 pieces graded so far. Even though many of these may be regrades as producers try to upgrade these gems, Norfolks can not escape being the commonest commemorative in gem to choice gem grades.

No issue has more 67 or 68 specimens when PCGS and NGC populations are combined. In addition, Norfolks are likely to have beautiful toning from original mint packaging. But what makes Norfolks the highest quality commemorative is their design. There is really no open area to show marks and hairlines as the design is even busier than a Texas. Where there would be unprotected fields, the Norfolk has a sculptured surface which protects these areas as well. The most likely trouble spot is on the ship's sails where sometimes a cut or two can be detected. Norfolks that do not grade 65 are probably coins that have been mishandled or cleaned. As you might expect, this issue has a very high basal value and, until 66, carries no significant premium over MS60. With the high basal value, MS66 coins represent good value for the collector. MS67 coins take a jump as supply finally starts to drop off. Investors will probably focus here. MS68 coins are available and currently trade for around $2,000.

- ✓ Do not purchase this coin below 65.
- ✓ Frosty white gems are available in every grade and quite common in 65 and 66.
- ✓ Mini hoards do exist and many investors have several examples because of the availability and relatively low price of choice specimens.
- ✓ Author's choice: *Collector* MS66; *Investor* MS67.

Harry Laibstain

Oregon Trail
1926

Mintage
Business strikes: 47,955
Ranking: (112)

Certified Populations & Historical Values

	MS60	MS62	MS63	MS64	MS65	MS66	MS67
Pop.	4	61	431	1,040	584	122	13
Rank	(109)	(103)	(107)	(110)	(85)	(76)	(81)
Pricing							
1957	—	—	$ 5	—	—	—	—
1970	—	—	12	—	—	—	—
1980	$ 115	—	160	—	$ 240	—	—
1982	85	—	115	—	165	$ 330	—
1989	90	$ 110	160	$ 250	750	2,300	$ 3,700
1994	80	90	110	155	210	486	1,500

Percent of mintage certified...5%
Popular collector grades................................MS63-65   Popular investor grades..................................MS65-67
Background: Commemorate the Oregon Trail and the heroism of those who traversed it

Comments

The 1926 Oregon Trail and its sister coin, the '26-S, are the first in a series of 14 coins widely acclaimed for their beautiful designs. They are very highly collected and are probably the most interesting commemorative set, as the coins represent 8 different dates spanning 14 years. Unlike other commemorative multi-year issues which usually revolve around PDS sets, these coins were issued as singles for four years and double issues for two years. Oregons were only produced as traditional PDS sets in 1938 and 1939.

The 1926-P Oregons are available in grades up to MS65 in frosty white condition. MS66 coins often exhibit some toning or a light patina. The strike is usually bold and the surfaces do not suffer the die polishing problems of the 1926-S. The 1926-P has the second highest mintage among Oregons and trades as a type coin in grades up to 65. This was not always the case as 1926-P Oregons, in MS65, had carried a premium. 1926-P Oregons do not come as nice, nor were they preserved as well as the lower-mintage, later-date issues. Their population rankings in MS65 to 67 reflect this. Even though its rarity in MS65 is greater than or equal to eight other Oregons, the 1926-P still trades as type. The 1926-P does carry some premium in 66 and 67. However, it is still underrated in these grades. This issue suffers from of a high mintage in a series with many low mintages and an abundance in low grades.

TIPS!

✓ Current price levels do not accurately reflect the value of this coin in high grades.
✓ Stay away from heavy or mottled toning in this issue.
✓ Avoid cuts on the Indian's chest and leg.
✓ Author's choice: *Collector* MS65; *Investor* MS66. This issue is Highly Recommended.

Oregon Trail
1926-S

Mintage
Business strikes: 83,055
Ranking: (121)

Certified Populations & Historical Values

	MS60	MS62	MS63	MS64	MS65	MS66	MS67
Pop.	5	83	502	1,173	883	277	61
Rank	(112)	(108)	(115)	(114)	(119)	(114)	(127)
Pricing							
1957	—	—	$ 4	—	—	—	—
1970	—	—	12	—	—	—	—
1980	$ 115	—	160	—	$ 240	—	—
1982	85	—	115	—	165	$ 330	—
1989	90	$ 110	160	$ 250	700	2,175	$ 2,800
1994	80	85	105	155	210	442	1,050

Percent of mintage certified..4%
Popular collector grades...MS63-65   Popular investor grades................................MS65-67
Background: Commemorate the Oregon Trail and the heroism of those who traversed it

Comments

The 1926-S has the highest mintage of the Oregon Trail series. Population rankings are consistent throughout the grade range varying from 108 to 127. Only 4% of this issue has been certified. Many 1926-S Oregons are found in circulated condition or low-grade mint state. The 1926-S can have incredible flashy luster but often suffers from die polishing problems. The coins are available white but many have some degree of toning that, when mixed together with the intense luster, can create a beautiful coin. Many of the coins graded 66 and 67 have this combination working for them.

The 1926-S trades as common up to grade 65 and is a very popular type coin. In 66 it is quite a bit scarcer than several of the later low-mintage issues and suffers some of the same stigmas as the 1926-P. This issue, like all Oregon Trails, has strong demand and 65 and 66 grades should have room for growth. As long as 67 prices remain just above type prices, these represent good value as well.

TIPS!
- ✓ Buy this coin in grades 64 and above.
- ✓ Avoid coins with extreme die polishing.
- ✓ Pretty toned coins are available and command a moderate premium.
- ✓ Author's choice: *Collector* MS65; *Investor* MS66. This issue is Recommended.

Oregon Trail
1928

Mintage
Business strikes: 6,028
Ranking: (45)

Certified Populations & Historical Values

	MS60	MS62	MS63	MS64	MS65	MS66	MS67
Pop.	0	21	121	469	541	175	23
Rank	(1)	(67)	(53)	(69)	(80)	(90)	(100)
Pricing							
1957	—	—	$ 7	—	—	—	—
1970	—	—	16	—	—	—	—
1980	$ 250	—	300	—	$ 440	—	—
1982	190	—	265	—	400	$ 800	—
1989	170	$ 205	225	$ 325	1,400	2,475	$ 3,800
1994	140	150	155	230	300	560	1,600

Percent of mintage certified..................22%
Popular collector grades..........MS63-65   Popular investor grades..........MS65-67
Background: Commemorate the Oregon Trail and the heroism of those who traversed it

Comments

The 1928 is one of the scarcer Oregon Trail issues based on combined populations. Excluding the '39 PDS set, only one Oregon Trail has a lower MS65 ranking than the 1928. With its lower mintage and popular design, the 1928 Oregon is a better-date coin that is usually in demand and sells quickly.

This issue has some problems with luster but white coins are generally available up to grade 65. Sometimes the luster on the 1928's can be steely or flat. Early issues of any type are much more likely to suffer from mishandling and cleaning than later issues and the 1928 is no exception.

Pricing on this coin represents basal values up to grade 63. In 64 and 65 it carries a modest premium and current demand could support higher prices for nice specimens. In MS66 the current premium more accurately reflects the market. The MS67 population is low and these coins are rarely available. Over the years I have probably placed 6 of these and they are still in the hands of collectors. MS67 remain speculative but probably represent good value.

✓ Avoid coins with heavy hits on leg or chest areas.
✓ Coins with frosty white luster are scarcer than you might expect. Don't be afraid to pay moderate premiums.
✓ Do not purchase this issue below grade 64.
✓ Author's choice: *Collector* MS65; *Investor* MS67. This issue is Highly Recommended.

Oregon Trail
1933-D

Mintage
Business strikes: 5,008
Ranking: (30)

Certified Populations & Historical Values

	MS60	MS62	MS63	MS64	MS65	MS66	MS67
Pop.	0	3	116	558	584	135	13
Rank	(1)	(18)	(51)	(81)	(85)	(82)	(81)
Pricing							
1957	—	—	$ 10	—	—	—	—
1970	—	—	28	—	—	—	—
1980	$ 275	—	340	—	$ 550	—	—
1982	335	—	590	—	870	$ 1,750	—
1989	190	$ 220	250	$ 375	1,425	4,000	$ 5,100
1994	225	250	260	310	395	675	1,850

Percent of mintage certified..28%
Popular collector grades.................................MS63-65   Popular investor grades.................................MS65-67
Background: Commemorate the Oregon Trail and the heroism of those who traversed it

Comments

With its low mintage and sexy date, the 1933-D is a very popular coin. The U.S. Mint only produced a few coins in 1933 – cents from Philadelphia and Denver and halves from San Francisco. This issue is also the only commemorative with this date. 1933-D Oregon Trails generally come with white frosty luster. However, they often suffer from ticky bag marks that keep the number of gem specimens low.

Prices for 1933-D Oregon Trails have remained somewhat constant in grades up to MS64, mainly due to the coin's high basal value. For several years one well-known mail order dealer was willing to pay up to $300 for any specimen, thus capturing everything below 64 and sometimes low-end examples of those as well. This coin currently carries only a modest premium in 65 and nice examples are well worth the difference. MS66 coins nearly double in value and are still probably underrated at current levels. Until recently, 1933-D Oregons in MS66 were difficult to obtain. Although available sporadically, they sell quickly. MS67 coins are scarce and probably represent good value. Oregons are widely collected in the higher grades; I currently have two customers working on 67 sets.

✓ Avoid coins that are heavily marked.
✓ Expect to pay a premium for high-end cosmetic coins above grade 64.
✓ High basal value. Do not purchase below 64.
✓ Author's choice: *Collector* MS65; *Investor* MS66. This issue is Highly Recommended.

TIPS!

Harry Laibstain

Oregon Trail
1934-D

Mintage
Business strikes: 7,006
Ranking: (51)

Certified Populations & Historical Values

	MS60	MS62	MS63	MS64	MS65	MS66	MS67
Pop.	1	15	235	945	624	106	4
Rank	(66)	(45)	(84)	(105)	(90)	(69)	(54)
Pricing							
1957	—	—	$ 7	—	—	—	—
1970	—	—	12	—	—	—	—
1980	$ 210	—	300	—	$ 425	—	—
1982	150	—	230	—	365	$ 730	—
1989	170	$ 220	250	$ 375	1,575	4,200	$ 5,900
1994	140	155	170	220	345	725	2,300

Percent of mintage certified...28%
Popular collector grades...............................MS63-65   Popular investor grades....................................MS65-67
Background: Commemorate the Oregon Trail and the heroism of those who traversed it

Comments

The 1934-D Oregon Trail is similar to the 1933-D, although it is more common overall. With a moderate mintage for a multiple-year issue, the 1934-D does not hold the allure of the 1933-D. It's not until MS66 that the 1934 outperforms the other Oregon Trail issues. It is the scarcest Oregon issue in grades 66 and above. This coin suffers some quality problems such as poor color and bag marks, and it is difficult to find above-average quality for the grade. When PQ coins are available in the higher grades they should command a premium.

1934-D Oregons trade at basal value up to grade 63. MS64 and MS65 coins sell for a modest premium and nice examples are a good value for collectors. MS66 coins are underrated at today's levels and should increase nicely when commemorative prices rise in general. MS67 coins are rare and generally unavailable.

- ✓ Expect 64-66 graded coins to have some ticks.
- ✓ Do not purchase this coin below MS64.
- ✓ Strong investment potential in MS66.
- ✓ Author's choice: *Collector* MS65; *Investor* MS66. This issue is Highly Recommended.

Oregon Trail
1936

Mintage
Business strikes: 10,006
Ranking: (73)

Certified Populations & Historical Values

	MS60	MS62	MS63	MS64	MS65	MS66	MS67
Pop.	1	16	156	639	800	334	61
Rank	(66)	(49)	(73)	(92)	(111)	(120)	(127)
Pricing							
1957	—	—	$ 4	—	—	—	—
1970	—	—	12	—	—	—	—
1980	$ 130	—	175	—	$ 275	—	—
1982	110	—	150	—	260	$ 520	—
1989	150	$ 160	175	$ 250	700	1,785	$ 2,800
1994	110	110	120	155	220	336	1,050

Percent of mintage certified..20%
Popular collector grades..................................MS63-65 Popular investor grades..................................MS65-67
Background: Commemorate the Oregon Trail and the heroism of those who traversed it

Comments

With a mintage of 10,000, the 1936 Oregon Trail is relatively common for a multi-year issue. The population peaks in MS65 and there is no real shortage of 66 graded coins either. In the past, this was considered a better date. Today it essentially trades at type prices plus 5% in grades up through 66. MS67 coins carry a modest premium as their population falls somewhere in the middle of the other Oregon issues.

The 1936 Oregon comes nice and is often lightly and originally toned, but sometimes it can be dull. Most 1936 Oregons I have handled have been relatively free of marks but not really flashy. Eye-popping specimens should command at least a moderate premium. Untoned coins are available in grades up to 66 but most of the really white ones have been dipped. Ironically, these sell best. This issue is usually free of bag marks and strike is not a problem either. As long as prices remain close to type levels 1936 Oregons represent good value.

✓ Avoid coins with speckled or spotty toning or with dull surfaces.
✓ This issue should be priced very close to type prices.
✓ PQ 1936 coins are actually scarce as many other Oregon issues come with more eye appeal.
✓ Author's choice: *Collector* MS65; *Investor* MS66.

Harry Laibstain

Oregon Trail
1936-S

Mintage
Business strikes: 5,006
Ranking: (27)

Certified Populations & Historical Values

	MS60	MS62	MS63	MS64	MS65	MS66	MS67
Pop.	0	12	131	277	496	368	84
Rank	(1)	(34)	(59)	(27)	(75)	(126)	(133)
Pricing							
1957	—	—	$ 10	—	—	—	—
1970	—	—	16	—	—	—	—
1980	$ 200	—	300	—	$ 500	—	—
1982	165	—	275	—	475	$ 950	—
1989	200	$ 210	220	$ 350	750	1,550	$ 3,100
1994	125	150	160	200	300	440	900

Percent of mintage certified..27%
Popular collector grades.................................MS64-65 Popular investor grades...MS65-67
Background: Commemorate the Oregon Trail and the heroism of those who traversed it

Comments

The 1936-S Oregon Trail, with its low mintage and relatively low population rankings, is often a difficult coin to locate. MS64 and MS65 specimens are scarce in relation to their demand. Except for the ultra-low mintage 1939 set, the 1936-S has the lowest ranking of all Oregon Trails in 64 and 65. The reason the prices on these middle grades remain relatively low relates to the 66 and 67 populations.

This issue comes nice and tends to grade high, keeping a cap on the lower grades. Most coins I have seen tend to have sharp detail and good luster. Bag marks are minimal and untoned coins are available up to grade 66. Coins with attractive toning command a moderate premium.

The rankings in the highest grades should cause this coin to trade as common, but they do not. The moderate premium that begins in MS64 is retained all the way up the grading scale. This can be partially explained by the fact that the total mint state population is low and collectors of 64 and 65 coins may be purchasing 66 specimens. I have seen dealers advertising to pay 65-plus money for nice 64 coins because they could not locate them. Suffice to say that appealing mid-range specimens sell quickly.

- ✓ This issue is underrated below MS66 and often unavailable.
- ✓ Look for nice coins with eye appeal in this issue.
- ✓ Popular multi-year issue, subject to hoarding by collectors based on low mintage and availability.
- ✓ Author's choice: *Collector* MS64; *Investor* MS65. This issue is Recommended.

Oregon Trail
1937-D

Mintage
Business strikes: 12,008
Ranking: (83)

Certified Populations & Historical Values

	MS60	MS62	MS63	MS64	MS65	MS66	MS67
Pop.	1	20	126	384	995	931	308
Rank	(66)	(65)	(57)	(53)	(105)	(140)	(142)
Pricing							
1957	—	—	$ 4	—	—	—	—
1970	—	—	12	—	—	—	—
1980	$ 125	—	175	—	$ 275	—	—
1982	100	—	140	—	250	$ 500	—
1989	105	$ 155	175	$ 275	700	1,550	$ 2,800
1994	100	105	115	155	220	320	900

Percent of mintage certified...23%
Popular collector grades..............................MS64-66   Popular investor grades...............................MS65-68
Background: Commemorate the Oregon Trail and the heroism of those who traversed it

Comments

The 1937-D is the winner of the quality award in the Oregon Trail series. This coin comes gem more often than not and even boasts an MS68 population of 25. Although the population just barely escapes peaking in 66, the high rankings in this grade and in 67 further attest to its super quality. From grades 64 and up, this issue trades as a type coin and is several times more common than other Oregons trading similarly.

The 1937-D often comes with an incredibly thick, white luster. The Denver mint had evidently learned some things about coining Oregon Trails and would also go on to produce high quality examples in the next two years. This issue is not rare but the coins are so nice they often trade at a small premium. They are the Oregon that is most often purchased as a type in 65 and above, despite the lower mintage. There are three commemorative issues that show similar quality: the Norfolk, Iowa and York. They are the equivalent of the early S mint dollars of the Morgan series. Although ultra common in high grades, they will always be very popular.

- ✓ Expect this issue to be gem quality.
- ✓ Do not purchase below MS65.
- ✓ Super examples will trade at a premium even though rarities dictate otherwise.
- ✓ Author's choice: *Collector* MS66; *Investor* MS67.

Harry Laibstain

Oregon Trail
1938-P, D, S

Mintage
Business strikes: 6006, 6005, 6006
Ranking: (42) (41) (42)

Certified Populations & Historical Values

	MS60	MS62	MS63	MS64	MS65	MS66	MS67
38-P: Pop	0	11	139	446	649	242	46
Rank	(1)	(33)	(63)	(65)	(92)	(108)	(119)
38-D: Pop	0	7	95	289	669	532	125
Rank	(1)	(27)	(42)	(29)	(95)	(134)	(138)
38-S: Pop	0	17	102	399	677	362	62
Rank	(1)	(53)	(45)	(56)	(99)	(124)	(129)
Set Pricing							
1957	—	—	$ 20	—	—	—	—
1970	—	—	37	—	—	—	—
1980	$ 500	—	650	—	$ 850	—	—
1982	350	—	485	—	725	$ 1,450	—
1989	450	$ 545	600	$ 975	2,200	4,700	$ 8,400
1994	*600	*600	*610	620	750	*1,195	*3,400
Individual Pricing (1994)							
1938-P	$ 135	$ 140	$ 155	$ 185	$ 250	$ 400	$ 1,075
1938-D	150	165	175	210	250	350	900
1938-S	135	140	155	185	250	350	975

Percent of mintage certified..26%, 29%, 27%
Popular collector grades......................................MS63-65 Popular investor grades.................................MS65-67
Background: Commemorate the Oregon Trail and the heroism of those who traversed it

Comments

The 1938 PDS Oregon set was the first time all three mints got together on production of Oregon Trails. Although 1938 Oregons have a relatively low mintage, they are not as scarce as this would indicate. They are difficult to locate in grades 64 and below and trade for some premium over type in these grades. The premium starts to diminish in higher grades as populations and rankings increase. The 1938-P, while readily available in MS65, has a low population in 66 and is underrated in this grade. The 1938-D, which is scarce below 65, is the most common of the three above this level.

The Denver issue is the undisputed quality winner among the 1938 Oregons. Dealers trying to put together low-end uncertified sets have trouble locating the 1938-D because most available specimens have been certified 65 or better. Occasionally a cleaned 1938-D, which is uncertified, will fetch a 65 price. The 1938-S is equal in rarity to the P and D in 65. Even though its population is considerably smaller than the D in 66, it is not scarce enough to command a premium over it. This is a popular set, as are all Oregon Trails, and it is subject to hoarding. Listed prices had overstated set values for several years and single coins can be purchased at moderate premiums to type levels.

- ✓ Do not purchase these coins below MS64.
- ✓ Avoid dark or splotchy toned coins or coins with unappealing card toning.
- ✓ The '38-PDS Oregons are easily assembled one piece at a time and do not have to be purchased as a set. You should not have to pay significant premiums.
- ✓ Author's choice: *Collector* MS65; *Investor* MS66. These issues are Recommended.

Oregon Trail
1939-P, D, S

Mintage
Business strikes: 3004, 3004, 3005
Ranking: (11) (11) (13)

Certified Populations & Historical Values

	MS60	MS62	MS63	MS64	MS65	MS66	MS67
39-P: Pop	1	9	78	224	365	190	34
Rank	(66)	(28)	(32)	(17)	(56)	(97)	(115)
39-D: Pop	0	19	62	180	342	256	78
Rank	(1)	(62)	(21)	(5)	(48)	(110)	(132)
39-S: Pop	0	18	71	213	343	197	41
Rank	(1)	(59)	(27)	(13)	(49)	(98)	(117)
Set Pricing							
1957	—	—	60	—	—	—	—
1970	—	—	105	—	—	—	—
1980	825	—	1,100	—	1,350	—	—
1982	500	—	725	—	1,150	2,000	—
1989	1,200	1,325	1,400	1,725	4,150	7,000	8,600
1994	*1,250	*1,260	1,290	1,300	1,735	2,285	*7,100
Individual Pricing (1994)							
1939-P	$ 360	$ 365	$ 400	$ 425	$ 575	$ 750	$ 2,000
1939-D	375	385	430	450	585	725	1,550
1939-S	360	365	400	425	575	750	1,750

Percent of mintage certified..30%, 31%, 30%
Popular collector grades.............................MS63-65 Popular investor grades.................................MS65-67
Background: Commemorate the Oregon Trail and the heroism of those who traversed it

Comments

The 1939 Oregons have the lowest mintage in the Oregon series. Because of this and the overall popularity of Oregon Trails, low-grade specimens are worth almost as much as some higher grades. Ungradeable sets trade in the $1,000 to $1,100 range, which is not far from MS63 prices. The low populations in grades up to 64 help explain the high basal value of these coins. In higher grades, the low mintage tends to conflict with the population rankings. 1939 Oregons are not exceptionally rare in grades 65 and above. It is clear that these issues were widely saved as collectors believed that the low mintages would lead to big profits. In addition, all three mints were turning out a quality product. 1939 Oregons usually have smooth, unmarked surfaces with good luster and good strikes. Untoned coins are available up to grade 66 and come in varying degrees of whiteness. Some coins were saved in original cards and acquired beautiful toning which enhanced their desirability.

1939 Oregons have fairly consistent population rankings in relation to one another. The D mint is the highest quality product of the three and is difficult to locate in lower grades or for uncertified sets. Conversely, in the higher grades it is the most com-

Harry Laibstain

1939-P, D, S Oregon Continued

mon. The P and S mints have similar population rankings in all grades, with the P mint being just a little more difficult to locate above 65. These three issues represent the scarcest of all the Oregons in 65 with rankings from 19 to 27 points better than the next closest (1936-S).

Although available in grades 65 and higher, these coins are not as common as their populations would indicate. 1939 Oregons may be the most hoarded of all commemoratives. I have one customer with nearly 50 sets. The low mintage and high basal value will continue to attract collectors and investors and keep pressure on their price levels. Appealing 1939 Oregons sell quickly in all grades and I expect they will continue to do so.

- ✓ High basal value; do not purchase these below grade 64.
- ✓ Lightly toned or white coins are available. Avoid dark toning or unappealing card toning.
- ✓ May be the most hoarded of all commemoratives.
- ✓ Author's choice: *Collector* MS65; *Investor* MS66. These issues are Highly Recommended.

Panama-Pacific
1915-S

Mintage
Business strikes: 27,134
Ranking: (108)

Certified Populations & Historical Values

	MS60	MS62	MS63	MS64	MS65	MS66	MS67
Pop.	23	325	609	717	350	133	28
Rank	(134)	(133)	(120)	(96)	(50)	(81)	(108)
Pricing							
1957	—	—	$ 45	—	—	—	—
1970	—	—	70	—	—	—	—
1980	$ 775	—	1,750	—	$ 4,800	—	—
1982	285	—	600	—	1,825	$ 3,200	—
1989	280	$ 475	950	$ 2,150	6,100	13,600	$27,500
1994	250	425	570	1,030	2,220	3,720	8,000

Percent of mintage certified..8%
Popular collector grades................................MS62-64 Popular investor grades.................................MS64-67
Background: Commemorates the opening of the Panama Canal

Comments

The Pan-Pac half is one of the earliest silver commemoratives, part of the important Panama-Pacific five-piece set that includes four gold commemoratives. Pan-Pac halves have a moderate mintage for non-PDS issues. These coins were subject to much mishandling and cleaning and tend to grade low overall. The result can be seen in the low rankings in grades up to 63. Above MS63, Pan-Pac rankings take a curious twist. They get a little tougher in 64, rank 46 points higher in 65 and then in, 66 and 67, the relative scarcity begins to decrease. The rankings drop back 31 points in MS66 and an additional 26 points to 108 in MS67.

Pan-Pacs, when properly preserved, are extremely nice coins. Many have pretty and colorful toning while other examples exist with blazing white to satiny white luster. If this issue were coined 20 years later and handled the way coins in the '30's were, many more gems would exist today. Pan-Pacs are available untoned up to grade 65. Above 65 you should expect attractive toning. Lower-grade coins from 62 to 64 with positive eye appeal sell quickly and usually at moderate/strong premiums over current listings. Pan-Pac prices have not decreased since 1989 by the same percentages as other commemoratives of similar rarity. High-grade specimens, like 65 and 66, are probably fully valued at present. The relatively high population of 67 graded coins makes them speculative at current levels. Compare prices closely before purchasing.

✓ Purchase coins from this issue with good eye appeal and be ready to pay a premium for nice coins in lower grades.
✓ Toning is common on this issue, particularly around the periphery, just inside the rim.
✓ Avoid cleaned (washed out) or splotchy dark-toned coins which are common.
✓ Author's choice: *Collector* MS64; *Investor* MS65. This issue is Recommended.

Harry Laibstain

Pilgrim
1920

Mintage
Business strikes: 152,112
Ranking: (133)

Certified Populations & Historical Values

	MS60	MS62	MS63	MS64	MS65	MS66	MS67
Pop.	19	406	1,233	1,712	696	115	6
Rank	(128)	(138)	(139)	(134)	(102)	(73)	(62)
Pricing							
1957	—	—	$ 5	—	—	—	—
1970	—	—	15	—	—	—	—
1980	$ 60	—	90	—	$ 225	—	—
1982	46	—	64	—	170	$ 340	—
1989	47	$ 65	120	$ 525	2,300	6,400	$ 9,200
1994	60	62	70	140	625	1,500	6,000

Percent of mintage certified..3%
Popular collector grades...MS63-64 Popular investor grades...MS65-66
Background: 300th anniversary of the landing of the Pilgrims at Plymouth Rock, Massachusetts

Comments

The 1920 Pilgrim is the more common of this two-year issue. Low-grade specimens are extremely plentiful, as evidenced by the low rankings in grades up to 64. Although relatively common in 64, it doubles in value from the previous grade. This is partly due to the higher value of 65 coins, which take a huge jump from 64's. After MS64, the Pilgrim gets progressively tougher as the grade gets higher. Even though this coin is considered common by most collectors, it does have significant grade rarity at the upper end. An MS66 1920 Pilgrim is worth more than a Spanish Trail in the same grade, though a 63 Spanish Trail is worth almost 10 times that of a 63 Pilgrim.

Pilgrims do have some quality problems. There are large open field areas on the obverse and the portrait is raised sufficiently to pick up marks. The reverse is often weakly struck, particularly in the center sails and mast area. In addition this early issue, like so many others, was subject to mishandling. This coin essentially trades at basal value up to 63. Nice 63 and 64 coins are a good value and sell quickly. MS65 examples are popular with investors and sell almost as well. Because of the grade rarity, 66 and 67 coins remain speculative. Grade rarity was very popular in the 1980's. It remains to be seen whether that will be the continuing trend.

- ✓ Do not purchase this coin below 63.
- ✓ NGC 65 examples trade at a 10%-25% discount to PCGS coins and nice NGC pieces are probably a bargain.
- ✓ Don't expect Pilgrims to be defect-free in any grade. The design suffers from numerous quality problems.
- ✓ Author's choice: *Collector* MS64; *Investor* MS65. This issue is Recommended.

Pilgrim
1921

Mintage
Business strikes: 20,053
Ranking: (97)

Certified Populations & Historical Values

	MS60	MS62	MS63	MS64	MS65	MS66	MS67
Pop.	3	127	423	927	451	55	4
Rank	(100)	(115)	(105)	(101)	(68)	(52)	(54)
Pricing							
1957	—	—	$ 12	—	—	—	—
1970	—	—	55	—	—	—	—
1980	$ 160	—	250	—	$ 490	—	—
1982	130	—	200	—	435	$ 870	—
1989	105	$ 135	220	$ 700	2,825	7,700	$10,000
1994	80	110	145	245	820	2,150	7,500

Percent of mintage certified..10%
Popular collector grades...................................MS62-64 Popular investor grades.................................MS65-66
Background: 300th anniversary of the landing of the Pilgrims at Plymouth Rock, Massachusetts

Comments

The 1921 is the scarcer of the two Pilgrims, with a fairly consistent population ranking up to grade 64. The coin is somewhat scarce in these lower grades, particularly when compared to non-PDS issues. In higher grades it becomes increasingly tougher, exhibiting a similar pattern to the previous year's issue. 1921 Pilgrims suffer from the same quality problems as the 1920 and, additionally, often have die-polishing problems on the obverse. The degree of severity fluctuates but those from one die have extreme die polish covering the open fields. This "variety" was thought to be scarce at one time but does not command any premium. In fact, the grading services often view these die polished coins critically because of the negative eye appeal caused by the raised lines.

1921 Pilgrims are in demand and sell quickly in grades up to 66. White coins are available in grades up to 65; above 65 they usually have some toning. This coin is underrated in grades up to 64. MS65 and MS66 examples are probably accurately priced with current demand supporting these levels. Because of the extremely low populations of 67 coins, it's hard to determine an accurate value. Purchases at this level should be considered speculative.

- ✓ Popular issue which is not part of the 50-piece type set.
- ✓ Do not purchase below MS63.
- ✓ Specimens with strong eye appeal and smooth surfaces should command a moderate premium.
- ✓ Author's choice: *Collector* MS64; *Investor* MS65. This issue is Highly Recommended.

Harry Laibstain

Rhode Island
1936-P, D, S

Mintage
Business strikes: 20013, 15010, 15011
Ranking: (94)   (87)   (88)

Certified Populations & Historical Values

	MS60	MS62	MS63	MS64	MS65	MS66	MS67
36-P: Pop	3	51	401	1,197	924	201	5
Rank	(100)	(95)	(104)	(117)	(120)	(102)	(57)
36-D: Pop	3	52	334	944	726	172	8
Rank	(100)	(97)	(99)	(104)	(104)	(88)	(69)
36-S: Pop	3	61	374	859	527	77	2
Rank	(100)	(103)	(102)	(98)	(78)	(59)	(44)
Set Pricing							
1957	—	—	$ 25	—	—	—	—
1970	—	—	45	—	—	—	—
1980	$ 500	—	650	—	$ 975	—	—
1982	265	—	320	—	475	$ 950	—
1989	300	$ 320	345	$ 1,350	5,100	18,900	$27,500
1994	195	201	210	285	975	3,690	15,300
Individual Pricing (1994)							
1936-P	$ 65	$ 67	$ 70	$ 95	$ 320	$ 1,075	—
1936-D	65	67	70	95	320	1,075	—
1936-S	65	67	70	95	335	1,750	—

Percent of mintage certified..14%, 15%, 13%
Popular collector grades...MS64-65   Popular investor grades....................................MS65-66
Background: 300th anniversary of the founding of Providence, Rhode Island

Comments

This single-year set has a relatively high mintage for PDS issues. The Philadelphia mint coin with its higher mintage has somewhat lower rankings than its mintmarked counter parts. This becomes more obvious as the grade increases through MS66. The San Francisco issue proves to be scarcer above 63 than the Denver coin even though their mintages are the same. As the grade increases, the difference becomes larger. This is probably best explained by production quality. The D mint was a better product and tends to grade higher. The primary difference is mint bloom. The three issues suffer some quality problems but nice coins can usually be located. Some specimens exhibit noticeable die polishing or bubbly surfaces. However, these problems are not usually obvious enough to detract from the overall grade although they may affect eye appeal.

All Rhode Islands price the same up to grade 64 and the S mint commands a small premium in 65. This will vary depending on the quality. High quality S mints in 65 sometimes bring strong premiums because of the increased spread generated by the much more valuable MS66 S mints. Rhode Islands are available untoned in grades up to 65 and sometimes 66. The highest grades usually exhibit some toning and often it is colorful. Prices up to grade 65 are reasonable and current demand is in line with prices. MS66 Rhode Islands represent condition rarity and are probably fully priced at this time. MS67 populations are really too low to analyze values and should be considered speculative.

✓ Rhode Islands with colorful toning command moderate to strong premiums in 64 and 65 and moderate premiums in 66.
✓ Due to the busy design, most small bag marks are well hidden. Avoid coins with large obvious cuts.
✓ The Philadelphia issue is available proof-like, although virtually no contrast can be seen between the fields and devices.
✓ Author's choice: *Collector* MS64; *Investor* MS65.

TIPS!

Roanoke
1937

Mintage
Business strikes: 29,030
Ranking: (110)

Certified Populations & Historical Values

	MS60	MS62	MS63	MS64	MS65	MS66	MS67
Pop.	2	59	363	1,523	1,998	717	187
Rank	(93)	(101)	(101)	(128)	(140)	(138)	(140)
Pricing							
1957	—	—	$ 12	—	—	—	—
1970	—	—	23	—	—	—	—
1980	$ 150	—	235	—	$ 460	—	—
1982	130	—	180	—	275	$ 550	—
1989	220	$ 230	250	$ 325	925	2,325	$ 5,000
1994	160	170	180	190	215	350	1,700

Percent of mintage certified..17%
Popular collector grades..................................MS64-66 Popular investor grades.................................MS65-67
Background: 350th anniversary of the colonization of Roanoke Island, North Carolina

Comments

This historic issue has a moderate/high mintage and is also one of the top five quality issues, very common in gem condition. Roanoke's have a high basal value and, up to grade 64, all MS coins are worth about the same. In 65, Roanokes carry a small premium over this level. Based on its basal value, nice 65 specimens are a good buy for the collector.

Roanokes grade high for a variety of reasons. The design is very busy with inscriptions and has few unprotected fields. On the obverse, the most susceptible areas are the face and hat. On the reverse, cuts are sometimes picked up in the skirt. The luster on this issue is generally high and exhibits a cartwheel effect like a Morgan dollar. These coins were issued in cards and many display attractive toning over lustrous surfaces. Toned Roanokes can be quite beautiful and many of the 66's and 67's are like this.

Although common, Roanokes are in demand. Not only are they part of the 50-piece type set but they enjoy strong regional demand and interest from history buffs. In addition, many commemorative collectors have more than one Roanoke because of its high quality. Current pricing up to 66 is accurate as long as basal value stays where it is. MS67 coins seem pricey in relation to 66's and their high population puts added pressure on current levels.

- ✓ Roanokes may be accompanied by original cards, literature and envelopes which are valuable.
- ✓ Generally seen as flashy white coins, some with very intense luster.
- ✓ Demand quality in this issue, avoid any large cuts in the face or hat.
- ✓ Author's choice: *Collector* MS65; *Investor* MS66.

Harry Laibstain

Robinson - Arkansas
1936

Mintage
Business strikes: 25,265
Ranking: (106)

Certified Populations & Historical Values

	MS60	MS62	MS63	MS64	MS65	MS66	MS67
Pop.	7	158	812	1,461	749	200	15
Rank	(114)	(118)	(130)	(124)	(106)	(101)	(86)
Pricing							
1957	—	—	$ 11	—	—	—	—
1970	—	—	21	—	—	—	—
1980	$ 125	—	225	—	$ 375	—	—
1982	100	—	130	—	205	$ 410	—
1989	90	$ 110	130	$ 300	1,850	5,500	$ 9,600
1994	60	65	70	110	315	1,210	4,100

Percent of mintage certified...14%
Popular collector grades.................................MS63-65 Popular investor grades.................................MS65-66
Background: New obverse design for the Arkansas Centennial

Comments

The Robinson has a moderate mintage and is generally considered a common type issue, particularly in the lower grades. Below MS64, the coin trades near basal value as a result of its availability. From 64 on, this issue develops a handsome premium and makes a large percentage jump between each grade. Like many issues that are common in the middle grades, the Robinson/Arkansas has condition rarity at the higher levels. This is partly due to the obverse design. Nearly the entire obverse is open and susceptible to cuts and scrapes. Even the device of the senator's head is large with flat surfaces, so these coins did not preserve well. The luster is generally good on this issue, although some pieces are subdued. It is this latter group which is likely to be the cleanest looking. A light toning haze or patina will tend to fill in tiny scrapes and lines – I have seen many Robinsons that benefited from this effect.

Robinsons are fairly priced. MS64 coins represent excellent value for the collector and 65 coins are lower than one might think considering their population. MS66 coins, while fairly priced for their population, do not have as strong a demand as other single issues. Prices for 67 coins, although $5,500 lower than in 1989, still seem too high.

- ✓ Avoid coins with serious obverse cuts and scrapes, particularly in the face and head.
- ✓ Do not expect this coin to be perfect; some light friction and marks are acceptable, even in higher grades. Many 66 coins I have seen have some light but noticeable obverse friction.
- ✓ Mini hoards may exist.
- ✓ Author's choice: *Collector* MS64; *Investor* MS65. This issue is Recommended.

San Diego
1935-S

Mintage
Business strikes: 70,132
Ranking: (118)

Certified Populations & Historical Values

	MS60	MS62	MS63	MS64	MS65	MS66	MS67
Pop.	3	75	677	2,853	5,614	831	37
Rank	(100)	(106)	(125)	(143)	(144)	(139)	(116)
Pricing							
1957	—	—	$ 7	—	—	—	—
1970	—	—	13	—	—	—	—
1980	$ 65	—	90	—	$ 175	—	—
1982	58	—	76	—	160	$ 320	—
1989	85	$ 95	110	$ 175	550	2,425	$ 4,800
1994	53	55	60	65	80	250	1,910

Percent of mintage certified..............14%
Popular collector grades................MS64-66   Popular investor grades................MS65-67
Background: Souvenir for the San Diego, California – Pacific Exposition

Comments

The 1935-S San Diego half dollar has the distinction of being the most common commemorative in MS65. With almost 6,000 pieces graded, the population exceeds its nearest competitor (1936-D San Diego) by almost 2,000 coins. It just misses a similar honor in 64 as only the Stone Mountain has a higher population in this grade. This trend continues to 66, where the '35-S is the 6th most common. In 67 the ranking rises 23 places and generates a huge leap in value.

San Diegos obviously come extremely nice. Most coins that I see are white with strong luster. This issue will often suffer from some light ticks and scrapes, mostly on the obverse, which is probably why its population peaks in 65 rather than 66. White coins are readily available through MS66 with most 67 graded specimens having some colorful, attractive toning.

1935-S San Diegos below grade 65 are inexpensive and likely to stay that way. In fact, coins graded 64 and lower essentially trade at basal value. In 65 this issue carries a very modest premium and nice specimens represent a good buy for the collector. MS66 coins triple in value from 65 prices, influenced partly by the extremely high prices of 67's. MS66 coins are reasonably priced but 67's seem too high at almost 8 times the price of a 66 and 24 times the price of a 65. Insist on an incredible coin before purchasing a high-priced MS67 specimen.

✓ Do not purchase this issue below 65.
✓ Obverse is more likely to have noticeable marks than the reverse. Look for them in the skirt, chest and stomach area.
✓ This issue is often used for promotions and direct mail offerings.
✓ Author's choice: *Collector* MS65; *Investor* MS66.

TIPS!

Harry Laibstain

San Diego
1936-D

Mintage
Business strikes: 30,092
Ranking: (111)

Certified Populations & Historical Values

	MS60	MS62	MS63	MS64	MS65	MS66	MS67
Pop.	0	23	314	2,035	3,835	334	14
Rank	(1)	(72)	(95)	(141)	(143)	(120)	(84)
Pricing							
1957	—	—	$ 8	—	—	—	—
1970	—	—	15	—	—	—	—
1980	$ 110	—	150	—	$ 275	—	—
1982	75	—	115	—	210	$ 420	—
1989	95	$ 110	125	$ 180	675	3,200	$ 6,200
1994	55	60	65	68	90	322	2,800

Percent of mintage certified..22%
Popular collector grades.................................MS64-66 Popular investor grades..................................MS65-67
Background: Souvenir for the San Diego, California – Pacific Exposition

Comments

The 1936-D San Diego is similar to the 1935-S. Like the 1935-S, it has extremely low rarity rankings in grades 64 and 65, being third and second most common, respectively. It is somewhat scarcer in 66 and 67 and price differences reflect this. Coins grading below 64 are represented by their basal value, with 64 coins being worth an extra $5-$10. With only a 10% to 15% price premium in 65, the 1936-D has almost 2,000 fewer coins than the 1935-S. 1936-D San Diegos are available untoned in grades up to 66. MS67 coins are usually attractively toned.

This issue is appropriately priced in the lower grades and is likely to stay where it is. MS65 and MS66 coins, currently a fraction of their previous highs (off 85-90%), will probably not reach those lofty levels anytime soon. These drops represent the largest declines of any coins of the commemorative series. MS65 populations may have grown too plentiful over the last 5 years and price levels will be constantly burdened with their availability. MS66 coins, however, are not that plentiful and increased demand coupled with promotions (common on these issues) could exert some price growth in the future.

- ✓ Considerably scarcer than 1935-S in gross numbers, although pricing is similar.
- ✓ Hoards may exist, populations could further increase.
- ✓ This issue is often used for promotions and direct mail offerings.
- ✓ Author's choice: *Collector* MS65; *Investor* MS66.

Sesquicentennial
1926

Mintage
Business strikes: 141,120
Ranking: (131)

Certified Populations & Historical Values

	MS60	MS62	MS63	MS64	MS65	MS66	MS67
Pop.	31	614	1,355	962	121	5	0
Rank	(137)	(142)	(140)	(106)	(11)	(6)	(1)
Pricing							
1957	—	—	$ 10	—	—	—	—
1970	—	—	14	—	—	—	—
1980	$ 50	—	85	—	$ 150	—	—
1982	35	—	60	—	200	$ 400	—
1989	50	$ 75	275	$ 2,125	8,750	20,000	$30,000
1994	60	75	135	400	4,560	19,000	28,000

Percent of mintage certified..:2%
Popular collector grades................................MS62-64   Popular investor grades.................................MS64-65
Background: 150th anniversary of the Declaration of Independence.

Comments

The Sesquicentennial half dollar is an historic coin, part of a two-coin set that includes a $2.50 commemorative gold issue of the same date. The Sesqui has a very high mintage but is hard to locate in grades 63 and above. It's the ultimate example of grade rarity, with a ranking of 4th from the bottom in grades 63 and below. Then it jumps to a moderate ranking in 64 and is ultimately one of the scarcest commems in grade 65 and above. Its ranking of 11th in 65 would be 3rd if PDS coins were taken out of the equation. Only the Grant/Star and Missouri 2X4 have lower 65 populations and both are from two-coin issues. Therefore, the Sesqui in 65 is the rarest single-coin issue in the commemorative series (see *Tables 5 & 6*). Its rarity is similar in 66 and the coin does not exist in 67.

Sesquis are hard to find nice because they suffer from numerous quality problems: tiny marks are almost always found on the cheek (obverse) and bell (reverse). In addition, luster and coloration problems are numerous on this issue. When Sesquis do have full luster, it has an incredible intensity; unfortunately examples like this are the exception. Unappealing or splotchy toning is the rule. In fact, some coins of this issue are downright ugly. Even with all these potential hazards, white coins are available, though not plentiful, up through grade 64 and occasionally 65. Some toning should be expected on higher grades.

Nice mid-grade coins (62-64) are a bargain at today's levels. When available with strong eye appeal, these coins sell quickly at a premium. The spread between 64 and 65 is extremely enticing to upgraders. It is not unusual for high-end 64 Sesquis to trade for multiples of bid among knowledgeable dealers. MS65 coins with eye appeal are difficult to locate due to too much technical grading and overgraded coins which are the result of numerous resubmissions. When nice 65 Sesquis are encountered they bring premiums over listed prices, even though they are already among the most expensive commems in this grade. MS66 coins are seldom available and, at current prices, are highly speculative.

✓ Demand for this issue in high grade with eye appeal continues to outstrip supply. Expect to pay a premium for these.
✓ Nice MS64 coins are a favorite target of upgraders. Perhaps as many as 1/3 of the MS65's in holders today were once 64's.
✓ An ultimate example of grade rarity. MS65 coins are worth almost 40 times MS63 price.
✓ Author's choice: *Collector* MS64; *Investor* MS65. This issue is Highly Recommended.

Harry Laibstain

Spanish Trail
1935

Mintage
Business strikes: 10,008
Ranking: (76)

Certified Populations & Historical Values

	MS60	MS62	MS63	MS64	MS65	MS66	MS67
Pop.	1	33	236	831	940	285	25
Rank	(66)	(83)	(86)	(97)	(122)	(115)	(103)
Pricing							
1957	—	—	$ 55	—	—	—	—
1970	—	—	200	—	—	—	—
1980	$ 850	—	1,125	—	$ 1,900	—	—
1982	475	—	600	—	900	$ 1,800	—
1989	650	$ 675	725	$ 1,125	2,750	4,400	$ 5,100
1994	650	665	690	710	820	1,300	3,100

Percent of mintage certified..24%
Popular collector grades................................MS63-65   Popular investor grades................................MS65-67
Background: 400th anniversary of the Cabeza de Vaca Expedition through the Gulf states

Comments

The Spanish Trail has always been a favorite of commemorative collectors. This issue's low mintage (tied for 5th of non-PDS issues) coupled with its lack of availability in lower grades, gives it a high basal value. Any mint state example is currently worth between $600 and $700, making it the second most expensive commem in low grade after the Hawaiian. Even lightly circulated or mishandled examples trade around $600. Spanish Trails do not become plentiful until MS64 and the population peaks in 65. Despite its design, this coin can be considered a high quality issue. It has large open field areas but does not usually come scarred up. The luster is usually strong and many coins exhibit a thick frosting. Although most Spanish Trails are relatively clean, one or two bad marks in the field can cost the coin a grade because they are so noticeable. White coins are readily available in grades up to 65 but less often in 66. Higher grade specimens tend to have some toning or a light patina. Most 67 coins will usually have exceptional toning.

The Spanish Trail's value in grades up to 64 is represented by its high basal value. MS65 coins carry a small to moderate premium and are a good buy for collectors. In 66 Spanish Trail prices take their first real jump. These coins are also in demand at current levels and sell well. Even MS67 coins seem reasonably priced although declines from 1989 have not been great compared with other commems.

- ✓ Avoid coins with streaky color or washed out surfaces.
- ✓ 2nd highest basal value, do not purchase below 65.
- ✓ Counterfeits do exist, avoid uncertified purchases.
- ✓ Author's choice: *Collector* MS65; *Investor* MS66. This issue is Recommended.

Stone Mountain
1925

Mintage
Business strikes: 1,314,709
Ranking: (142)

Certified Populations & Historical Values

	MS60	MS62	MS63	MS64	MS65	MS66	MS67
Pop.	35	451	1,894	3,118	1,578	349	65
Rank	(139)	(139)	(144)	(144)	(137)	(122)	(130)
Pricing							
1957	—	—	$ 4	—	—	—	—
1970	—	—	10	—	—	—	—
1980	$ 30	—	45	—	$ 90	—	—
1982	28	—	36	—	80	$ 160	—
1989	30	$ 45	65	$ 165	750	1,815	$ 4,100
1994	30	32	37	62	160	615	2,000

Percent of mintage certified..1%
Popular collector grades.................................MS63-65 Popular investor grades................................MS65-67
Background: To raise funds for carving figures of Confederate leaders on Stone Mountain, Georgia

Comments

The Stone Mountain is one of the commemorative series most common coins. It has an extremely high mintage and high population in almost all grades. In grades below 63 this coin trades at or near basal value but 64 coins take a moderate jump and are always in demand. This issue has the highest certified population in 63 and 64. Surprisingly, not many coins from these grades linger on the market. A combination of low values and strong regional and historic demand keep supply balanced. MS65 coins take another nice jump in price as rarity starts to increase. MS66 and MS67 prices increase dramatically, causing this relatively common issue to have some big price spreads. There is some basis for this in the population figures. Although ranked near the bottom in 65, there are 22 issues in MS66 that have higher populations. When all PDS commem issues are combined as type coins, MS66 Stone Mountains rank 31st out of 50 (see *Table 10*).

Stone Mountains are available untoned in grades up through 65 and occasionally 66. Most high-grade specimens have some toning. Cuts and other abrasions are most often found down Lee's leg or on the horse on the obverse. Reverse problems occur in the open field area and on the eagle's body. Prices for Stone Mountains in the lower grades are low and stable at this time. In 65, nice specimens are in demand by collectors and investors and current prices are accurate. MS66 and MS67 levels, which at first glance appear pricey for a common coin, are not unreasonable. If this coin had a higher basal value (i.e. was rarer in the lower grades), these prices would seem more accurate and maybe even too low considering their populations.

TIPS!

✓ Avoid splotchy, dark-toned or off-color specimens, which are common in this issue.
✓ Due to the large mintage it is likely some mini hoards exist.
✓ Strong demand keeps these from glutting the market. Nice specimens of the most common grades are not always available.
✓ Author's choice: *Collector* MS64; *Investor* MS65. This issue is Recommended.

Harry Laibstain

Texas
1934

Mintage
Business strikes: 61,143
Ranking: (116)

Certified Populations & Historical Values

	MS60	MS62	MS63	MS64	MS65	MS66	MS67
Pop.	1	73	397	1,298	941	171	21
Rank	(66)	(105)	(103)	(121)	(123)	(87)	(96)
Pricing							
1957	—	—	$ 6	—	—	—	—
1970	—	—	15	—	—	—	—
1980	$ 80	—	105	—	$ 175	—	—
1982	80	—	105	—	175	$ 350	—
1989	115	$ 130	170	$ 250	650	1,550	$ 3,350
1994	75	76	80	85	135	240	1,150

Percent of mintage certified..5%
Popular collector grades..MS64-66 Popular investor grades..................................MS65-67
Background: 100th Anniversary of Texas' independence

Comments

The 1934 Texas was the first and only single-issue coin of the type. It also has the highest mintage of all 13 issues. Texas commemoratives are extremely popular due to strong regional demand and the attractive design. If all the years and dates of Texas (MS65) were added together, they would exceed the most common non-PDS issue by more than 3,000 coins. Breaking down multi-year and PDS issues bestows additional rarity, which is deserved by some more than others. Most commemorative collectors collect by type and therefore demand is actually higher for a single issue where no substitutes are available.

The 1934 Texas does not come as nice as the later PDS issues. Quality differences are most apparent in the higher grades. The mintage of the 1934 is roughly double the combined mintage of the three 1935 issues, yet its 65 population is just 40% of the combined 1935 MS65 populations. This difference is even more obvious in 66 when you compare 1934 populations to other Texas issues. At one time an MS66 1934 Texas carried a significant premium because of its low population, but not anymore. In grades 65 and below, this issue trades at type levels. In 66 and above, it carries premiums that are smaller than it deserves, particularly in 66.

✓ Currently a very small premium on 66 and 67 graded coins, all other grades trade as type.
✓ The issue lacks popularity because of its high mintage compared to the other issues.
✓ Try to buy attractive coins in higher grades. These are underrated when sold at type prices.
✓ Author's choice: *Collector* MS65; *Investor* MS66. This issue is Recommended.

Texas
1935-P, D, S

Mintage
Business strikes: 9996, 10007, 10008
Ranking: (70) (74) (76)

Certified Populations & Historical Values

	MS60	MS62	MS63	MS64	MS65	MS66	MS67
35-P: Pop	0	13	108	372	804	563	107
Rank	(1)	(39)	(47)	(49)	(112)	(136)	(134)
35-D: Pop	0	18	88	395	868	502	77
Rank	(1)	(59)	(35)	(55)	(116)	(132)	(131)
35-S: Pop	3	19	147	462	762	267	25
Rank	(100)	(62)	(68)	(68)	(107)	(112)	(103)
Set Pricing							
1957	—	—	$ 11	—	—	—	—
1970	—	—	42	—	—	—	—
1980	$ 240	—	325	—	$ 550	—	—
1982	240	—	300	—	490	$ 980	—
1989	345	$ 405	510	$ 750	1,950	4,575	$ 9,675
1994	225	228	240	276	450	775	**2820
Individual Pricing (1994)							
1935-P	$ 75	$ 76	$ 80	$ 92	$ 150	$ 225	$ 950
1935-D	75	76	80	92	150	225	950
1935-S	75	76	80	92	150	225	1,100

Percent of mintage certified...20%, 19%, 17%
Popular collector grades..MS64-66 Popular investor grades...MS65-67
Background: 100th Anniversary of Texas' independence

Comments

The 1935 Texas coins have moderately high mintages for multi-coin issues. In addition, two of the three issues come extremely nice which ensures a large supply of high-grade coins. Even though the S mint is considerably scarcer in grades above 65, it does not develop a premium until 67 and even then it is modest.

1935 Texas come with intense, frosty luster and usually have good strikes. Texas commems are rarely baggy but when cuts are found they will normally be in the centers on either side. The eagle's chest is especially prone to marks or scrapes, and imperfections here often cost a grading point. The reverse design is extremely busy with hardly any open fields. With its great luster and strike the reverse is almost always gem.

The three 1935 Texas are generally considered quite common and trade as type coins only. Prices in grades up to 63 represent basal value with 64 graded coins carrying a modest premium. In 65 this issue takes a jump and in 66 a similar increase. These levels are low by historical standards and represent good value and limited downside for the collector or investor. MS67 coins take a jump as populations are low relative to other grades. It is likely that purchases of Texas commems in 67 are more for type than for date collectors and current levels may be too high on the most common issues.

- ✓ Untoned coins are available through grade 66 and sometimes 67.
- ✓ Purchase only high-quality examples whether buying white coins or toned examples. These come nice.
- ✓ The MS67 1935-S could probably support a larger premium.
- ✓ Author's choice: *Collector* MS65; *Investor* MS66.

Harry Laibstain

Texas
1936-P, D, S

Mintage
Business strikes: 8911, 9039, 9055
Ranking: (61) (63) (64)

Certified Populations & Historical Values

	MS60	MS62	MS63	MS64	MS65	MS66	MS67
36-P: Pop	0	16	108	458	847	395	48
Rank	(1)	(49)	(47)	(66)	(115)	(127)	(121)
36-D: Pop	0	13	88	336	834	679	119
Rank	(1)	(39)	(35)	(39)	(114)	(137)	(137)
36-S: Pop	1	17	100	478	812	262	23
Rank	(66)	(53)	(44)	(71)	(113)	(111)	(100)
Set Pricing							
1957	—	—	$ 12	—	—	—	—
1970	—	—	42	—	—	—	—
1980	$ 240	—	325	—	$ 550	—	—
1982	245	—	315	—	515	$ 1,030	—
1989	345	$ 405	510	$ 750	1,950	4,600	$ 9,675
1994	225	228	240	276	450	*840	*3240
Individual Pricing (1994)							
1936-P	$ 75	$ 76	$ 80	$ 92	$ 150	$ 225	$ 975
1936-D	75	76	80	92	150	225	975
1936-S	75	76	80	92	150	225	1,150

Percent of mintage certified...21%, 23%, 19%
Popular collector grades................................MS64-66   Popular investor grades.................................MS65-67
Background: 100th Anniversary of Texas' independence

Comments

Almost everything said about the 1935 Texas holds true for the 1936 set. Although the '36 mintages are about 10% smaller, there is very little difference in populations. Like the 1935 set, the S mint from 1936 is noticeably scarcer in the highest grades than the other two. However, it only develops a premium in 67 and then it is modest. 1936 Texas coins tend to be a little more frosty white than 1935 issues but the coins run the gamut in both years and many look remarkably similar.

1936 Texas issues are readily available untoned in grades up through 66 and sometimes 67. When purchasing Texas commems in high grades you should expect good luster and a near complete absence of bag marks. Though relatively common in high grades, Texas commems are among the most beautiful and highly collected coins from the entire series. Prices up to grade 66 are modest and represent good value for commemorative enthusiasts.

- ✓ Texas commems are often available with multicolored toning and these coins command a premium.
- ✓ Do not purchase this issue with dull luster or excessive marks.
- ✓ These 3 are type coins and do not trade at date premiums.
- ✓ Author's choice: *Collector* MS65; *Investor* MS66.

Texas
1937-P, D, S

Mintage
Business strikes: 6571, 6605, 6637
Ranking: (46) (47) (48)

Certified Populations & Historical Values

	MS60	MS62	MS63	MS64	MS65	MS66	MS67
37-P: Pop	0	19	113	393	608	223	33
Rank	(1)	(62)	(50)	(54)	(88)	(105)	(112)
37-D: Pop	0	14	85	342	740	316	33
Rank	(1)	(42)	(33)	(42)	(105)	(118)	(112)
37-S: Pop	1	13	93	341	687	297	25
Rank	(66)	(39)	(39)	(40)	(101)	(117)	(103)
Set Pricing							
1957	—	—	$ 15	—	—	—	—
1970	—	—	45	—	—	—	—
1980	$ 300	—	400	—	$ 600	—	—
1982	265	—	350	—	575	$ 1,150	—
1989	395	$ 435	550	$ 750	1,950	4,600	$ 9,675
1994	225	235	255	300	480	*840	3,240
Individual Pricing (1994)							
1937-P	$ 75	$ 78	$ 85	$ 100	$ 160	$ 250	$ 1,040
1937-D	75	80	85	100	160	250	1,000
1937-S	75	78	85	100	160	250	1,200

Percent of mintage certified..21%, 23%, 22%
Popular collector grades.................................MS64-66 Popular investor grades.................................MS65-67
Background: 100th Anniversary of Texas' independence

Comments

1937 Texas sets have a low to moderate mintage for PDS issues. Because of this they are a little scarcer than the previous two sets, although the similarities outweigh the differences. The three coins have consistent populations in relation to each other. The pops are lower than 1935 or 1936 Texas issues, a difference commensurate with the lower mintages. Production quality among these issues was similar. 1937 Texas commems come with an intense luster, and on average, have slightly better strikes than 1935 and 1936 issues. They carry a small premium in price over the earlier issues. These premiums had been even greater but, as populations increased, it became apparent that they were only slightly scarcer than their higher mintage counterparts. The 1937 Texas are collected primarily as type but also by date collectors. In addition, the mintages are low enough to attract some hoarders, which helps increase demand. Like the earlier issues, prices are moderate and a small premium over type probably represents an accurate reflection of rarity.

✓ Texas commems carry a modest premium when purchased as a matched set. These coins must have similar coloration.
✓ 1937's are slightly better than common and represent good value when purchased at type prices.
✓ Expect high quality in this issue. Untoned coins are available up to 66. MS67 specimens usually have some toning.
✓ Author's choice: *Collector* MS65; *Investor* MS66. This issue is Recommended.

Harry Laibstain

Texas
1938-P, D, S

Mintage
Business strikes: 3780, 3775, 3814
Ranking: (17) (18) (19)

Certified Populations & Historical Values

	MS60	MS62	MS63	MS64	MS65	MS66	MS67
38-P: Pop	1	16	127	294	363	112	16
Rank	(66)	(49)	(58)	(30)	(54)	(71)	(87)
38-D: Pop	0	12	93	216	437	172	28
Rank	(1)	(34)	(39)	(14)	(67)	(88)	(108)
38-S: Pop	1	18	66	249	390	199	27
Rank	(66)	(59)	(24)	(24)	(60)	(99)	(107)
Set Pricing							
1957	—	—	$ 52	—	—	—	—
1970	—	—	95	—	—	—	—
1980	$ 575	—	700	—	$ 900	—	—
1982	320	—	500	—	825	$ 1,650	—
1989	525	$ 625	725	$ 900	3,275	5,900	$ 9,675
1994	450	585	*780	*825	*1020	1,485	*7200
Individual Pricing (1994)							
1938-P	$ 150	$ 175	$ 185	$ 225	$ 325	$ 650	$ 2,500
1938-D	150	175	200	250	325	425	1,575
1938-S	150	175	185	225	325	410	1,575

Percent of mintage certified..25%, 25%, 25%
Popular collector grades................................MS63-65   Popular investor grades..................................MS64-67
Background: 100th Anniversary of Texas' independence

Comments

The 1938 Texas set is the scarcest and most interesting of all the Texas issues. Because of their low mintage these coins have been aggressively collected and hoarded. The high percentages certified attest to how these were saved. As you might expect, 1938 issues have a high basal value and any mint-state coin is worth twice what a common Texas sells for. The influence of this coin's basal value extends to MS64. In 65 and 66 prices take a moderate jump, except the P mint, which takes a large jump. 1938-P Texas commems have noticeably lower populations than the D and S in grades 65 and above. In 66 the difference is great enough for a large premium.

Whether these 3 coins are collected as part of the 144-piece set, a Texas-only set or by low-mintage enthusiasts, they are usually collected together. The discrepancy between populations in 66 puts intense price pressure on the P mint as collectors with D and S coins try to complete their sets. This same situation exists for MS67 coins.

The 1938 Texas issues are available untoned up to grade 65 and often 66. They are similar in quality to the earlier sets as the populations still peak in 65. Nice specimens in all grades sell quickly. Many of our customers have multiples of these sets and continue to buy more when available. Nice untoned specimens are impossible to keep in inventory and we try to purchase all we can. 1938 Texas sets could probably support higher price levels based on current demand. In grades through 66 they have good growth potential.

TIPS!

✓ 1938 Texas commemoratives benefit from the combined demand of 3 different types of set builders and low mintage enthusiasts.
✓ They are often found as matched sets and usually with some toning. Attractive sets command moderate premiums.
✓ Heavily hoarded issue. Many collectors own multiples.
✓ Author's choice: *Collector* MS65; *Investor* MS66. This issue is Highly Recommended.

Fort Vancouver
1925

Mintage
Business strikes: 14,994
Ranking: (86)

Certified Populations & Historical Values

	MS60	MS62	MS63	MS64	MS65	MS66	MS67
Pop.	7	185	562	907	535	128	18
Rank	(114)	(125)	(119)	(100)	(79)	(79)	(90)
Pricing							
1957	—	—	$ 60	—	—	—	—
1970	—	—	74	—	—	—	—
1980	$ 525	—	750	—	$ 1,300	—	—
1982	320	—	500	—	850	$ 1,700	—
1989	320	$ 365	450	$ 850	4,300	7,600	$10,900
1994	200	250	320	450	950	2,350	6,250

Percent of mintage certified..16%
Popular collector grades................................MS63-64 Popular investor grades..................................MS65-67
Background: 100th anniversary of Fort Vancouver, Washington

Comments

With its low mintage and high-basal value the Vancouver has been a longtime favorite of commemorative collectors. One of the scarcer single-issue commemoratives, it enjoys moderate rankings in the lower grades and becomes tougher as the grade increases.

Vancouvers can have a strong luster and sometimes this combines with toning to produce extremely attractive coins. Many of the higher grade examples have some toning; therefore, white coins when available, usually command a premium. Vancouvers do suffer some quality problems and it is not always easy to locate specimens with eye appeal. One problem is unattractive toning. The other is high point friction on the shoulder or face (obverse) or on the frontiersman's back leg (reverse).

By historical standards, Vancouvers are inexpensive in grades below 65 even though declines have been moderate. This issue enjoys a strong basal value which supports these grades. Low mintage, single issues, price from the bottom up and Vancouvers below 65 are unlikely to decline any further. MS64 coins are a bargain for collectors. MS65 coins, now priced about $1,000, are hard to locate. The current market may be undervaluing this grade. By comparison, 66 coins seem to be more appropriately priced as the percent price decline since 1989 is smaller than MS65's. This is a tough coin to locate and nice specimens are probably worth the money. MS67 coins are hard to locate but seem pricey.

- ✓ White coins usually command a premium in grades 64 and above. This issue is also available with attractive toning. Vivid colorful specimens also command nice premiums.
- ✓ Single-issue mintage ranking of 4th. Single-issue population ranking of 11th in MS65 (see *Tables 2 & 8*).
- ✓ Popular coin with investment potential, particularly in 65.
- ✓ Author's choice: *Collector* <u>MS64</u>; *Investor* <u>MS65</u>. This issue is <u>Highly Recommended</u>.

Harry Laibstain

Vermont
1927

Mintage
Business strikes: 28,142
Ranking: (109)

Certified Populations & Historical Values

	MS60	MS62	MS63	MS64	MS65	MS66	MS67
Pop.	9	236	898	1,222	621	129	7
Rank	(118)	(129)	(131)	(118)	(89)	(80)	(65)
Pricing							
1957	—	—	$ 20	—	—	—	—
1970	—	—	32	—	—	—	—
1980	$ 250	—	385	—	$ 925	—	—
1982	180	—	240	—	475	$ 950	—
1989	180	$ 215	275	$ 725	3,275	7,350	$ 9,600
1994	125	132	170	275	900	1,680	7,000

Percent of mintage certified..11%
Popular collector grades................................MS63-64 Popular investor grades.................................MS65-67
Background: 150th anniversary of the battle of Bennington and the independence of Vermont

Comments

The Vermont has many similarities to the Vancouver and, because of their alphabetical proximity, they are often thought of together. Although the Vermont's mintage is almost double that of the Vancouver, their grade rarities form a similar trend. Vermonts are a little more common in every grade except for MS67 and have a significantly lower basal value, catching up in 65. Despite nearly identical populations in 66, there is a large price discrepancy between the two issues. This would not be all that noteworthy except 65 prices of the two issues are nearly the same. I believe 66 Vermonts are underrated and current market conditions could support a higher price level.

Vermonts are considered attractive by many but suffer some quality problems. The design is raised and the high points take much abuse, particularly on the obverse. Ira Allen's cheek and jaw line are the most susceptible area. On the reverse, the cat's outer legs, body and field area under the body are most likely to pick up cuts and ticks. In addition, Vermonts often have unappealing toning (discoloration). It is difficult to locate white Vermonts above grade 63 because some toning is often needed to camouflage the light lines and scratches that frequently occur. Many high-grade Vermonts would loose a point or two if it were not for this film or skin on the coin's surface.

Coins below 63 are represented primarily by basal value. MS63 and MS64 coins are moderately priced and are an excellent value for the collector. MS65's are in demand by investors and difficult to locate. Sometimes off-quality, unattractive coins linger on the market but nice examples sell quickly. Current demand for 65 and, to a greater extent, 66-graded coins could probably support higher price levels. With a population of just 7, MS67 coins are rare and command a big premium. Investment at this level is speculative.

✓ White coins command a premium and are rather scarce in this issue in grades 64 and above.
✓ Some nice 64's have more eye appeal than many 65's.
✓ Avoid specimens with unappealing, splotchy or stainy toning, which plague this issue.
✓ Author's choice: *Collector* MS64; *Investor* MS65. This issue is Highly Recommended.

TIPS!

Booker T. Washington
1946-P, D, S

Mintage
Bus. strikes: 1,000,546 / 200,113 / 500,279
Ranking: (141)   (135)   (137)

Certified Populations & Historical Values

	MS60	MS62	MS63	MS64	MS65	MS66	MS67
46-P: Pop	1	12	196	990	924	199	12
Rank	(66)	(34)	(79)	(107)	(120)	(99)	(79)
46-D: Pop	1	9	86	594	542	127	10
Rank	(66)	(28)	(34)	(89)	(81)	(78)	(72)
46-S: Pop	0	12	150	940	875	184	20
Rank	(1)	(34)	(69)	(103)	(117)	(93)	(94)
Set Pricing							
1957	—	—	$ 2	—	—	—	—
1970	—	—	8	—	—	—	—
1980	$ 30	—	35	—	$ 45	—	—
1982	33	—	40	—	60	$ 120	—
1989	30	$ 42	48	$ 75	500	1,075	$ 4,650
1994	30	36	42	50	120	486	**3000
Individual Pricing (1994)							
1946-P	$ 10	$ 12	$ 14	$ 16	$ 40	$ 160	$ 1,500
1946-D	10	12	14	16	40	162	1,500
1946-S	10	12	14	16	40	160	1,000

Percent of mintage certified ....<1%, 1%, <1%
Popular collector grades ....MS64-65   Popular investor grades MS65-67
Background: Commemorates the teachings of Booker T. Washington

Comments

The 1946 Booker T. Washington halves have the highest mintage and are the most common of all the BTW's. In fact, 1946 BTW commems are the highest mintage of all PDS sets based on total number of sets possible. Due to high mintages and low values, only a small percentage of these coins have been graded. Consistent with the mintage figures, the Denver coin is the scarcest while the P and S have similar populations. Despite this difference, all three coins trade as type. The D may be occasionally more difficult to locate and if you want it "now" you may have to pay a modest premium.

1946 BTW's are available untoned in grades up to 66. Many 66 graded coins have some toning and virtually every 67 I have seen was toned. Even more than other BTW's, the 1946 issues suffer from light ticks and scrapes, mainly on the obverse. But their higher mintages seem to offset this fact and ensures a ready supply of high-grade coins. These coins are the least expensive commemoratives in the series in grades up to 66, except for the MS66 Iowa. 1946 BTW's are scarcer in 66 than quite a few other issues but their low basal value and lack of strong demand in this grade keeps prices down.

✓ Do not purchase these issues in certified grades below 65. Raw 64's can be purchased for $15.
✓ Untoned coins are most popular in these issues, although vividly toned coins do command moderate to large premiums depending on the issue's value.
✓ Good place to start collecting commems because of low prices.
✓ Author's choice: *Collector* MS65; *Investor* MS66.

Harry Laibstain

Booker T. Washington
1947-P, D, S

Mintage
Bus. strikes: 100,017 / 100,017 / 100,017
Ranking: (123)   (123)   (123)

Certified Populations & Historical Values

	MS60	MS62	MS63	MS64	MS65	MS66	MS67
47-P: Pop	0	1	16	312	268	10	0
Rank	(1)	(8)	(4)	(33)	(38)	(14)	(1)
47-D: Pop	0	0	28	218	176	9	0
Rank	(1)	(1)	(13)	(16)	(24)	(13)	(1)
47-S: Pop	0	3	29	238	364	24	0
Rank	(1)	(18)	(14)	(22)	(55)	(29)	(1)
Set Pricing							
1957	—	—	$ 8	—	—	—	—
1970	—	—	12	—	—	—	—
1980	$ 55	—	70	—	$ 90	—	—
1982	52	—	64	—	85	$ 170	—
1989	39	$ 45	55	$ 78	650	1,525	$ 4,650
1994	36	37	60	86	230	**1050	2,775
Individual Pricing (1994)							
1947-P	$ 12	$ 12	$ 20	$ 30	$ 60	$ 550	—
1947-D	12	12	20	28	120	750	—
1947-S	12	12	20	22	50	475	—

Percent of mintage certified ....1%, <1%, 1%
Popular collector grades..MS64-65   Popular investor grades..MS65-66
Background: Commemorates the teachings of Booker T. Washington

Comments

Like their 1946 counterparts, the 1947 BTW's suffer from the stigma of high mintages. Unlike the '46, their mintages do not create enough high-grade slabs to cause common rankings. 1947 BTW's are the scarcest of all BTW's in 65 and 66. Actual values for 66's reflect this scarcity, but 65 prices are low in comparison to availability. Pricing guides currently list 66 sets for less than what the singles are worth and 65's have suffered this misreporting in the past. Throughout the late '80's and up until present, many PDS-set prices have been misreported. This occurred primarily because prices were listed by set and the coins most often traded as singles.

Grades below 64 trade at this coin's basal value. MS64 coins do carry a modest premium and are sought by collectors. These issues are available untoned up to grade 65. MS66 specimens usually have some color and strong originality. Like other BTW's, these often suffer from ticks and scrapes on the obverse, particularly on the face and forehead.

1947 BTW's are sleepers in the commemorative series. Because BTW commems are exceptionally common overall, many collectors ignore them, leading to low prices. Even though populations are low, MS64 coins are unlikely to move up. If prices were to increase, raw coins, which are not worth submitting now, would be certified and satiate demand. The same cannot be said for 65 and 66 quality coins. These coins have very low populations (particularly 65's) in relation to their prices. Even a slight increase in demand could cause them to be worth more. Current demand for 65-graded coins can probably support higher prices.

✓ Ignored and underrated issues in high grade.
✓ White coins are popular in this issue but higher grade coins with light or attractive toning should be acceptable.
✓ This issue is common uncertified but most specimens range from AU to MS63 quality.
✓ Author's choice: *Collector* MS65; *Investor* MS65. This issue is Highly Recommended.

Booker T. Washington
1948-P, D, S

Mintage
Bus. strikes: 8005, 8005, 8005
Ranking: (54) (54) (54)

Certified Populations & Historical Values

	MS60	MS62	MS63	MS64	MS65	MS66	MS67
48-P: Pop	0	0	11	331	379	16	0
Rank	(1)	(1)	(2)	(38)	(58)	(21)	(1)
48-D: Pop	0	0	27	315	385	30	0
Rank	(1)	(1)	(12)	(35)	(59)	(35)	(1)
48-S: Pop	0	2	21	250	491	50	1
Rank	(1)	(15)	(7)	(25)	(74)	(49)	(27)
Set Pricing							
1957	—	—	$ 11	—	—	—	—
1970	—	—	17	—	—	—	—
1980	$ 90	—	135	—	$ 240	—	—
1982	88	—	1,128	—	205	$ 410	—
1989	66	$ 84	110	$ 275	700	1,200	$ 4,650
1994	77	80	85	*135	150	*750	2,775
Individual Pricing (1994)							
1948-P	$ 25	$ 26	$ 28	$ 30	$ 50	$ 240	—
1948-D	25	26	28	30	50	220	—
1948-S	25	26	28	30	50	200	—

Percent of mintage certified................9%, 9%, 10%
Popular collector grades.........MS64-65   Popular investor grades.........MS65-66
Background: Commemorates the teachings of Booker T. Washington

Comments

The 1948 BTW sets are the first of the low-mintage coins of this type. With a ranking of 54th, they have a moderate mintage for PDS coins but seem rare in comparison to the 1946 and 1947 sets. In grade 65 these coins are only scarcer than the 1946 and 1949 BTW sets (they price higher than the '46, lower than the '49). 1948 BTW's are high-quality issues with the S mint coming the nicest. The latter often has semi proof-like surfaces and is occasionally available in proof-like condition. The P and D also come nice and are usually found untoned with smooth fields. The usual problem is light abrasions on the obverse, where the coin is largely unprotected, particularly on the face and forehead.

1948 BTW prices are essentially basal value up to MS64. Price guides have listed 64 sets consistently higher than at the levels certified 64 coins actually trade. Strangely, raw sets tend to trade near these higher levels, causing them to be worth as much or more out of the holder. MS65 specimens trade at only modest premiums. With a value of just $50 in gem condition, these 40-year-old silver coins with mintages under 10,000 represent good value. Current demand can support higher values for these coins in 65 and some growth seems inevitable. MS66 prices jump 400% over 65 levels but still seem very reasonable, based on their populations and affordability.

- ✓ These issues are sometimes used for promotions and direct mail campaigns.
- ✓ Minimum grade recommended to purchase, MS65. Untoned coins most popular.
- ✓ All 3 issues trade as type up to grade 65.
- ✓ Author's choice: *Collector* <u>MS65</u>; *Investor* <u>MS66</u>. This issue is <u>Highly Recommended</u>.

TIPS!

Harry Laibstain

Booker T. Washington
1949-P, D, S

Mintage
Business strikes: 6004, 6004, 6004
Ranking: (36) (36) (36)

Certified Populations & Historical Values

	MS60	MS62	MS63	MS64	MS65	MS66	MS67
49-P: Pop	0	0	23	312	430	43	1
Rank	(1)	(1)	(9)	(33)	(64)	(47)	(27)
49-D: Pop	0	4	33	341	424	33	0
Rank	(1)	(21)	(16)	(40)	(63)	(39)	(1)
49-S: Pop	0	1	22	216	561	73	0
Rank	(1)	(8)	(8)	(14)	(83)	(58)	(1)
Set Pricing							
1957	—	—	$ 14	—	—	—	—
1970	—	—	30	—	—	—	—
1980	$ 175	—	240	—	$ 375	—	—
1982	155	—	200	—	330	$ 660	—
1989	78	$ 96	120	$ 340	700	1,700	$ 4,650
1994	165	165	180	190	225	605	3,900
Individual Pricing (1994)							
1949-P	$ 50	$ 50	$ 50	$ 55	$ 75	$ 195	—
1949-D	50	50	50	55	75	225	—
1949-S	65	65	65	65	75	185	—

Percent of mintage certified..13%, 14%, 15%
Popular collector grades..MS64-65 Popular investor grades..................................MS65-66
Background: Commemorates the teachings of Booker T. Washington

Comments

The 1949 issues have the lowest mintages of all the BTW's but they are not the scarcest. In fact, only the 1946 set has higher populations in 65. Additionally, this set has the highest basal value of all BTW issues. Uncertified low mint state specimens bring close to the prices of MS65 coins. This is particularly obvious in the case of the 1949-S, where an MS60 specimen is worth only a little less than a 65.

1949 issues have similar characteristics to the 1948 set. They are generally of very high quality, with the S mint being the best. 1949 BTW coins are available fully brilliant, or frosty white up to and including grade 66. Often high-grade BTW's, particularly 1949's, will have a rich original patina and some vivid toning. In other cases, rim toning that bleeds into the surface will display several mini rainbows. These coins tend to grade higher and command premiums over their standard brilliant counterparts.

Prices for 1949 BTW's come up from the bottom. The first real jump in prices is found in MS66 which, like 65's, are the most commonly graded BTW's except for the 1946 issues. Even so, this grade seems reasonably priced. Although their populations are a bit higher, the coins are still scarce and nice specimens are usually unavailable at current levels. With limited availability of quality coins and high basal values, these issues have growth potential.

TIPS!
- ✓ Expect 1949's to come nice whether fully brilliant or lightly toned.
- ✓ Do not purchase these issues below grade 65. The difference in quality is worth the difference in price.
- ✓ Matched sets and/or attractively toned coins from this set usually command small to moderate premiums, particularly in 65.
- ✓ Author's choice: *Collector* MS65; *Investor* MS66. This issue is Recommended.

Booker T. Washington
1950-P, D, S

Mintage
Bus. strikes: 6004 / 6004 / 512,091
Ranking: (36) (36) (139)

Certified Populations & Historical Values

	MS60	MS62	MS63	MS64	MS65	MS66	MS67
50-P: Pop	0	1	13	232	322	20	0
Rank	(1)	(8)	(3)	(20)	(44)	(24)	(1)
50-D: Pop	0	0	23	270	296	16	0
Rank	(1)	(1)	(9)	(25)	(40)	(21)	(27)
50-S: Pop	0	5	30	343	672	87	3
Rank	(1)	(25)	(15)	(43)	(96)	(63)	(47)
Set Pricing							
1957	—	—	$ 14	—	—	—	—
1970	—	—	25	—	—	—	—
1980	$ 135	—	175	—	$ 325	—	—
1982	120	—	158	—	295	$ 590	—
1989	75	$ 90	105	$ 250	675	1,425	$ 4,650
1994	*85	*85	*95	*105	135	*975	3,900
Individual Pricing (1994)							
1950-P	$ 25	$ 25	$ 30	$ 30	$ 48	$ 250	—
1950-D	25	25	30	30	48	325	—
1950-S	12	12	15	17	39	185	—

Percent of mintage certified ....10%, 10%, <1%
Popular collector grades...................................MS64-65   Popular investor grades..................................MS64-65
Background: Commemorates the teachings of Booker T. Washington

Comments

The 1950 is the first BTW set where one issue is common and the other two considerably scarcer. This is often confusing to collectors because PDS sets are priced together. The P and D-mint coins have the low mintages and similar population breakdown. Even though their mintage figures are identical to the '49's and their rarity is greater, their prices are lower. The '50-S, with a mintage of over half a million, is common with only the '46-P and S more plentiful.

1950 BTW's are similar in quality to the two preceding years. The P and D come with thick frosty luster and are available untoned up to 65. Occasionally, 66-graded coins are found without toning but this would be the exception. Most MS66 P and D issues have light toning or vivid color that caused them to grade at that level. Coins with pretty coloration command a premium. The S mint is the flashiest of the three pieces and it is available untoned up to 66, often with semi proof-like surfaces.

1950 BTW's also price from the bottom up until grade 65. In 65, all three issues manage a modest jump. The scarcer P and D issues are probably priced too low, especially when compared to pieces from '48 and '49 sets. With rankings of 44th and 40th respectively, and attractive low mintages, these two issues have good growth potential. Despite considerably higher prices, the same argument could be made for MS66 P and D coins, as their rankings rise approximately 20 places each between 65 and 66.

- ✓ Do not figure S mint issue as 1/3 value of set in any grade.
- ✓ This set's values seem to suffer because of mixed mintages. High mintage of the 50-S makes the other two issues appear more common than they are.
- ✓ '50-S is the second most common BTW in proof-like.
- ✓ Author's choice: *Collector* MS65; *Investor* MS66. This issue is Highly Recommended.

Harry Laibstain

Booker T. Washington
1951-P, D, S

Mintage
Business strikes: 510,082 / 7004 / 7004
Ranking: (138) (39) (39)

Certified Populations & Historical Values

	MS60	MS62	MS63	MS64	MS65	MS66	MS67
51-P: Pop	0	1	77	572	316	31	2
Rank	(1)	(8)	(30)	(82)	(42)	(36)	(44)
51-D: Pop	1	1	19	241	327	25	1
Rank	(66)	(8)	(5)	(23)	(45)	(30)	(27)
51-S: Pop	0	0	10	126	480	80	1
Rank	(1)	(1)	(1)	(1)	(73)	(61)	(27)
Set Pricing							
1957	—	—	$ 12	—	—	—	—
1970	—	—	25	—	—	—	—
1980	$ 110	—	160	—	$ 240	—	—
1982	85	—	122	—	190	$ 380	—
1989	65	$ 78	90	$ 225	650	1,575	$ 4,650
1994	*100	*105	*110	*120	135	**584	3,900
Individual Pricing (1994)							
1951-P	$ 12	$ 12	$ 15	$ 18	$ 40	$ 200	—
1951-D	30	30	35	35	50	250	—
1951-S	30	30	35	35	40	185	—

Percent of mintage certified ....<1%, 9%, 10%
Popular collector grades ....MS64-65   Popular investor grades MS65-66
Background: Commemorates the teachings of Booker T. Washington

Comments

The 1951 BTW set is like the 1950 set only the P mint has the high mintage instead of the S. Ironically, the P and D – with mintages that vary widely – have similar rankings in MS65 and 66. Only the high population of the P mint in 64 indicates its common status. The S mint is the highest quality of this set; so high that it trades as common in 65 and above, despite its low mintage. With the vast majority of coins sent in grading 65, this issue has the No. 1 ranking (of 144) in MS64. However, this is meaningless since many substitutes are available at a modest premium in MS65.

All 3 issues are available untoned up to grade 66. However, many of the P and D specimens have some toning at this level. 1951 BTW's, like earlier issues, are more likely to suffer from chatter on the obverse than the middle-year sets of 1948 and 1949. Overall, these issues come nice. The S mint is often semi proof-like, and proof-like designated specimens are available.

Values for 1951 BTW's reflect their basal value to grade 64. Above this, the coins begin to bring a premium. In 65 these premiums are small and should be well worth the difference to collectors. In 66 these issues take a large price jump. The P and D seem to be underrated at today's price levels and could probably support higher market values. The S mint, although it is a low-mintage issue, is too common to justify a higher price.

- ✓ All three coins have different rarity and value scales.
- ✓ High basal value for set. If the coins don't grade 65 they are not worth sending to be graded.
- ✓ Price/population ranking ratios make these and other BTW commems attractive. Inexpensive coins like BTW's are an excellent place to start collecting commemoratives.
- ✓ Author's choice: *Collector* <u>MS65</u>; *Investor* <u>MS66</u>. This issue is <u>Highly</u> <u>Recommended</u>.

Washington-Carver
1951-P, D, S

Mintage
Business strikes: 110,018 / 10,004 / 10,004
Ranking: (129) (71) (71)

Certified Populations & Historical Values

	MS60	MS62	MS63	MS64	MS65	MS66	MS67
51-P: Pop	1	12	94	329	97	14	1
Rank	(66)	(34)	(41)	(37)	(4)	(17)	(27)
51-D: Pop	0	3	62	375	164	7	0
Rank	(1)	(18)	(21)	(50)	(22)	(9)	(1)
51-S: Pop	0	0	20	301	467	38	1
Rank	(1)	(1)	(6)	(32)	(69)	(42)	(27)
Set Pricing							
1957	—	—	$ 10	—	—	—	—
1970	—	—	8	—	—	—	—
1980	$ 60	—	70	—	$ 95	—	—
1982	72	—	90	—	125	$ 250	—
1989	42	$ 60	80	$ 200	1,650	3,800	$ 9,000
1994	55	55	70	100	**405	**1350	6,900
Individual Pricing (1994)							
1951-P	$ 15	$ 15	$ 15	$ 35	$ 300	$ 1,000	—
1951-D	20	20	25	35	95	900	—
1951-S	20	20	25	25	50	400	—

Percent of mintage certified ....<1%, 6%, 8%
Popular collector grades.............................MS64-65   Popular investor grades.................................MS65-66
Background: Commemorate the accomplishments of Booker T. Washington and George Washington Carver

Comments

The 1951 W/C set has many interesting twists. The P-mint issue, while having a mintage of over 100,000, is one of the rarest commemoratives in 65. With a ranking of 4th this can be a very hard coin to locate. If NGC populations are excluded, it becomes the second rarest in the set following only the Grant/Star, which is priced about 20 times higher. The Denver example from this set is also a "better" date and has a fairly low MS65 ranking of 22nd. The final issue ('51-S) proves, once again, that mintage is not an absolute indication of rarity. It is the second most common W/C in 65. This set is often incorrectly valued by the price guides due to confusion surrounding the varying rarities of three different issues in several different grades. These issues as well as other PDS sets should be analyzed and reported singularly.

1951 W/C sets come with three distinct personalities. The '51-P, while readily available in low mint state grades (both certified and raw), is almost never available in gem condition. Most '51-P's I have seen suffer from numerous bag marks or discoloration, the result of mishandling. In addition, the luster on this issue is sometimes flat or brassy and frosty white coins with minimal marks are rare. Toned MS65 '51-P's are not nearly as popu-

1951-P, D, S Washington-Carver Continued

lar as white or lightly toned specimens. However, they still sell well at lower prices because demand is greater than supply. '51-P Washington-Carvers in 65 go in and out of inventory quickly and it's best to put a coin like this on a want list if you're serious about obtaining it.

The luster of '51-D's range from dull or gray to brilliant, and high quality examples can be located. Like all Washington-Carvers, '51-D's sometimes suffer from marks and scrapes on the obverse faces and bag marks on the unprotected fields of the reverse. The current premium is low (about twice common) on the '51-D. This coin, although not exceedingly rare, has a low enough price to ensure future growth potential.

The S mint comes extremely nice with intense cartwheel luster. In addition, many of these have fewer marks which explains why they grade so high. The S mint trades as a common type coin and gem examples are available.

MS64 coins trade at or near their basal set value. These are a bargain for collectors on a budget because of their extremely low prices. MS66 coins take large price jumps. It is important to note that NGC has certified a significantly larger number of all W/C dates in MS66 than PCGS. Prices for these issues are difficult to pinpoint because of set price reporting and population discrepancies. Careful research should be done before purchasing PCGS or NGC better-date 66 Washington-Carvers.

TIPS!

✓ Do not expect to assemble 65 sets at current set prices.
✓ '51-P issue, while underrated, is only worth the premium price if certified. Do not spend more then $20 - $25 on uncertified specimens unless you're confident they will certify MS65.
✓ Don't be misled by population and pricing in 66. NGC coins dominate the 66 populations, particularly on better dates, and may trade at significant discount to their PCGS counterparts.
✓ Author's choice: *Collector* MS64 (P) / MS65 (D & S); *Investor* MS65 (P & D) / MS66 (S). This issue is Highly Recommended.

Washington-Carver
1952-P, D, S

Mintage
Business strikes: 2,006,292 / 8,006 / 8,006
Ranking: (144)   (57)   (57)

Certified Populations & Historical Values

	MS60	MS62	MS63	MS64	MS65	MS66	MS67
52-P: Pop	2	20	332	1,492	799	95	0
Rank	(93)	(65)	(98)	(126)	(110)	(68)	(1)
52-D: Pop	0	4	61	360	139	1	0
Rank	(1)	(21)	(20)	(45)	(15)	(1)	(1)
52-S: Pop	0	1	23	382	362	33	1
Rank	(1)	(8)	(9)	(51)	(53)	(39)	(27)
Set Pricing							
1957	—	—	$ 12	—	—	—	—
1970	—	—	14	—	—	—	—
1980	$ 90	—	120	—	$ 210	—	—
1982	98	—	115	—	175	$ 350	—
1989	42	$ 60	80	225	1,800	3,800	$ 9,000
1994	60	65	90	105	**225	**1275	6,900
Individual Pricing (1994)							
1952-P	$ 12	$ 12	$ 15	$ 20	$ 50	$ 400	—
1952-D	25	25	30	35	170	2,000	—
1952-S	25	25	35	40	55	440	—

Percent of mintage certified ....<1%, 7%, 10%
Popular collector grades.............................MS64-65   Popular investor grades...............................MS65-66
Background: Commemorate the accomplishments of Booker T. Washington and George Washington Carver

Comments

The 1952 W/C issues are similar to the 1951 issues, except the '52-P is not rare in high grades. The '52-P is the highest mintage commemorative in the entire series, exceeding its closest competitor by almost half a million coins. As you might expect, it is also the most common W/C in 65 by over 300 examples. The '52-D is a low mintage issue and "better" date. With a combined population of 139 and a ranking of 15th, the '52-D is difficult to locate and trades at about three times common. The '52-S follows a similar pattern to the '51-S, as it has a low mintage but is actually quite common in high grade. It is the third most common W/C in 66 after the '52-P and '51-S.

The '52-P is available with white, brilliant luster in grades up to 65. Many high-grade '52-P's have original toning which ranges from attractive to dark. MS66 specimens almost always have some toning. '52-D specimens have weak luster and are commonly dull or steely gray in color. Frosty gem '52-D's are quite scarce and nice examples may command a premium over listed prices. '52-S specimens have intense full luster and are a better quality issue than either the P or D. Gem S mints, both toned and untoned, are generally available.

Harry Laibstain

1952-P, D, S Washington-Carver Continued

1952-P Carvers trade as type in every grade, with values sufficiently low that they have virtually no downside risk. The '52-D issue does trade at significant premiums in 65, but all lower grades are essentially represented by its basal value. This issue is scarce in 65 and generally unavailable at today's levels. It would only take a small increase in demand to propel this coin to higher levels. The '52-S has a strong basal value which carries through the entire grade range. Its 65 price is being pushed up from the bottom. Even though its 65 population is high enough to make it a type coin, the '52-S trades at a modest premium. Due to the small difference in prices I would not purchase this coin below 65.

- ✓ '52P & S coins can be found with attractive toning or color. Avoid dark or mottled examples.
- ✓ Set value is often misquoted because the three issues are distinct.
- ✓ '52-D & S issues have been used in mass promotions in both grades 64 & 65. Many coins are off the market.
- ✓ Author's choice: *Collector* MS65 (P & S) / MS64 (D); *Investor* MS66 (P & S) / MS65 (D).
    This issue is <u>Highly</u> <u>Recommended</u>.

Washington-Carver
1953-P, D, S

Mintage
Business strikes: 8,003 / 8,003 / 108,020
Ranking: (52) (52) (128)

Certified Populations & Historical Values

	MS60	MS62	MS63	MS64	MS65	MS66	MS67
53-P: Pop	0	1	89	361	129	7	0
Rank	(1)	(8)	(38)	(46)	(13)	(9)	(1)
53-D: Pop	0	4	64	371	87	1	0
Rank	(1)	(21)	(23)	(48)	(2)	(1)	(1)
53-S: Pop	0	2	60	540	369	32	1
Rank	(1)	(15)	(18)	(77)	(57)	(38)	(27)
Set Pricing							
1957	—	—	$ 11	—	—	—	—
1970	—	—	16	—	—	—	—
1980	$ 140	—	175	—	$ 250	—	—
1982	128	—	152	—	215	$ 430	—
1989	60	$ 65	80	$ 225	2,125	4,150	$ 9,000
1994	65	65	75	105	400	**1275	6,900
Individual Pricing (1994)							
1953-P	$ 25	$ 25	$ 30	$ 40	$ 125	$ 1,400	—
1953-D	25	25	30	40	225	2,250	—
1953-S	12	12	15	20	50	400	—

Percent of mintage certified..7%, 7%, 1%
Popular collector grades..MS64-65   Popular investor grades...............................MS65-66
Background: Commemorate the accomplishments of Booker T. Washington and George Washington Carver

Comments

The 1953 W/C issues have a similar mintage relationship to the 1952 set except that the S mint is the high mintage issue instead of the P mint. The P and D have virtually the same mintage as the D and S from 1952. As you can see from the rankings, both the P and D are significantly better dates with MS65 rankings of 13th and 2nd, respectively. The S mint is common and continues to follow the trend of 1951 and 1952 issues. The only difference is that the '53-S has a large mintage coupled with high quality and MS65 examples carry no premium whatsoever.

The 1953-P usually comes with nice frosty luster. Untoned coins comprise the vast majority of certified specimens. It is surprising that the 65 population of this issue is not higher. The quality may not be as strong as the S mints, but neither is it as poor as the D mints. The rarity of MS65 specimens can probably be attributed to this issue's low mintage and average production quality. This date is usually unavailable in high grades and, at current prices, is undervalued.

The '53-D is the scarcest Carver in 65, just inching out the

Harry Laibstain

1953-P, D, S Washington-Carver Continued

'51-P. The '51-P actually lists higher and is scarcer when NGC populations are excluded. '53-D coins tend to have poor luster and are often ticky. This can be a difficult coin to locate in 65, especially a nice example. Although this coin prices way above common, it is still cheap when compared with the larger commemorative series. Its ranking of 2nd in MS65, with a combined pop of only 87 and a price under $300 leaves it significant room for growth. This issue has been overlooked and is obviously undervalued.

The '53-S W/C is available untoned in grades up to 65 and occasionally 66 (most 66's have some toning). It trades at type levels in every grade and has almost no downside at current levels.

TIPS!

✓ Set prices often misquoted by pricing guides. All three issues should be listed separately.
✓ Don't expect '53-D to look like other P & S mint products even in the higher grades.
✓ Low mintage '53-P and '53-D coins have been used in promotions and many coins are currently held by individual collectors.
✓ Author's choice: *Collector* MS65; *Investor* MS65 (P & D) / MS66 (S). This issue is Highly Recommended.

Washington-Carver
1954-P, D, S

Mintage
Bus. strikes: 12,006 / 12,006 / 122,024
Ranking: (81) (81) (130)

Certified Populations & Historical Values

	MS60	MS62	MS63	MS64	MS65	MS66	MS67
54-P: Pop	0	2	88	483	158	16	0
Rank	(1)	(15)	(35)	(72)	(20)	(21)	(1)
54-D: Pop	1	4	97	443	108	4	0
Rank	(66)	(21)	(43)	(64)	(7)	(4)	(1)
54-S: Pop	20	5	144	573	356	27	0
Rank	(130)	(25)	(66)	(83)	(51)	(32)	(1)
Set Pricing							
1957	—	—	$ 10	—	—	—	—
1970	—	—	9	—	—	—	—
1980	$ 65	—	75	—	$ 95	—	—
1982	72	—	92	—	125	$ 250	—
1989	45	$ 60	80	$ 200	2,175	4,475	$ 9,000
1994	50	55	70	80	360	**1275	6,900
Individual Pricing (1994)							
1954-P	$ 19	$ 20	$ 22	$ 30	$ 130	$ 900	—
1954-D	19	20	22	30	175	2,000	—
1954-S	12	12	15	20	50	600	—

Percent of mintage certified..6%, 5%, 1%
Popular collector grades...MS64-65   Popular investor grades...MS65-66
Background: Commemorate the accomplishments of Booker T. Washington and George Washington Carver

Comments

The mintage relationship of the 1954 issues are similar to those of 1953 but a little more plentiful. The P and D are low-mintage better dates and the S mint is a common type coin with a high mintage. There is little difference in availability in grades below 65 and all three issues are moderately priced. In 65 the P mint (ranking 20th) and the D mint (ranking 7th) become relatively scarce, as their higher prices indicate. The '54-P is generally available untoned up to grade 65 and sometimes 66. This issue comes with strong luster and is probably the best P mint in that category. Its relationship to the '54-D is virtually the same as the '53-P to the '53-D. Although the mintage figures are the same, there are more high-grade P mints due to the difference in quality from each mint.

The '54-P is moderately priced for a coin with such a low population. Although I don't like it as much as the '53-P in 65, I still feel this coin has room for growth. Careful inspection shows us this coin's rarity is more in line with the '51-D while its price is most similar to '53-P. This is because 1954-P's in 65 were sold

Harry Laibstain

1954-P, D, S Washington-Carver Continued

in a promotion about two years ago, dispersing about half the population. Actual available supply and current demand are the main determinants of value. If coins are off the market, the issue is much harder to find than if they are floating around in dealer inventories.

The '54-D W/C is another tough-to-locate, underrated issue. Like the '52 and '53 Denver coins, the '54 issue does not come very nice. The luster is usually dull and sometimes a little gray. In addition, small ticks and bag marks are common. While coins are available up to grade 65, don't expect them to look like other higher quality issues. It is interesting to note that the '54-D is tied for 7th ranking in MS65 with the 38-S Arkansas. The Arkansas trades for four to five times the price of the '54-D; and it still represents excellent value. The better-date Carvers have been overlooked for too long and have tremendous potential for long-term growth.

The '54-S is available untoned in grades up to 65. MS66 examples usually have some toning. This issue has very good luster and usually fewer marks than the other two mints. Washington-Carver type prices are reasonable and provide another good place to start collecting commemoratives.

✓ Not necessary to purchase these coins as sets; most often found as singles.
✓ Set pricing can be misleading. Do research to help determine the value of each issue on any set where the rarities are different.
✓ NGC issues dominate 66 populations. Where this is the case NGC coins will trade at moderate to significant discounts to PCGS coins.
✓ Author's choice: *Collector* MS65; *Investor* MS65 (P & D) / MS66 (S). This issue is Highly Recommended.

Wisconsin
1936

Mintage
Business strikes: 25,015
Ranking: (100)

Certified Populations & Historical Values

	MS60	MS62	MS63	MS64	MS65	MS66	MS67
Pop.	0	41	299	1,232	2,129	991	161
Rank	(1)	(91)	(92)	(119)	(141)	(141)	(139)
Pricing							
1957	—	—	$ 14	—	—	—	—
1970	—	—	28	—	—	—	—
1980	$ 150	—	225	—	$ 450	—	—
1982	140	—	190	—	295	$ 600	—
1989	220	$ 240	275	$ 400	1,125	2,200	$ 4,250
1994	145	150	155	165	205	310	1,300

Percent of mintage certified..19%
Popular collector grades.................................MS64-66   Popular investor grades...................................MS65-67
Background: 100th anniversary of Wisconsin Territorial Government

Comments

The Wisconsin, with a moderate mintage, is one of the most common commemoratives in gem condition. In MS65 and 66 it ranks only 3rd from the bottom and in 67 only 5th from the lowest possible ranking. This issue illustrates how certification and population tracking have changed our perception of which coins are really rare.

The Wisconsin usually comes with a strong to slightly subdued luster. Although it has open field areas, bag marks are few and most specimens have only the lightest ticks or abrasions. Sometimes the badger will pick up a cut or scrape and occasionally some light chatter in the reverse field. Wisconsins are readily available untoned up to grade 66. Many have some light toning, which enhances their clean lustrous surfaces. These coins can usually be found in 66 and 67 holders.

Wisconsins have a fairly strong basal value which continues its influence up to grade 64. MS65 coins carry a small premium, and are a good value for the collector. The coin takes its first significant price jump in 66. Though this price is nearly 1/8th of its previous high, it is unlikely Wisconsins in 66 will reach this level again. In 1989, the number of slabbed coins did not sufficiently represent their actual availability. The Wisconsin in 66 is a lesson in hindsight for those who paid $2,200. At $300, nice 66 coins are probably a bargain and have room for growth. It is interesting to note that the 1982 price for 65 Wisconsins is about the same as the 1994 MS66 price. MS67 coins are not really rare as indicated by the population of 161. These coins are fully priced and could decline further as their population continues to grow.

✓ Do not be misled by huge 1989 prices; growth potential exists but not to that extent.
✓ Do not purchase this coin below 65; expect a coin with good eye appeal.
✓ Coins with outstanding luster or colorful toning command a premium in this high-quality issue.
✓ Author's choice: *Collector* MS65; *Investor* MS66. This issue is Recommended.

TIPS!

York
1936

Mintage
Business strikes: 25,015
Ranking: (100)

Certified Populations & Historical Values

	MS60	MS62	MS63	MS64	MS65	MS66	MS67
Pop.	3	52	352	1,084	1,898	1,158	362
Rank	(100)	(97)	(100)	(111)	(139)	(142)	(143)
Pricing							
1957	—	—	$ 10	—	—	—	—
1970	—	—	24	—	—	—	—
1980	$ 150	—	240	—	$ 540	—	—
1982	120	—	165	—	240	$ 480	—
1989	220	$ 240	250	$ 385	1,050	1,900	$ 3,175
1994	140	140	150	160	190	225	875

Percent of mintage certified..20%
Popular collector grades.................................MS64-66 Popular investor grades.................................MS65-68
Background: 300th anniversary of York County, Maine

Comments

The York is another high-quality commemorative. It shares many similarities with the Wisconsin and coincidently follows it in the series alphabetically. Like the Vermont and Vancouver, these coins are often thought of together. In addition, both issues have the same mintage and date. Above MS64 the population rankings are almost identical, with the York just a few ranking points more common overall.

Like the Wisconsin, Yorks come extremely nice. With its busy design, the coin is susceptible to visible cuts and scrapes only on the obverse shield and in the small unprotected field areas. Significant marks in these areas can cost a York a grade point. The mint luster of Yorks is usually way above average. Most high-grade original specimens exhibit a white luster with a thick rich frost. Even coins that have been dipped look nice and can qualify for the highest grades.

Yorks have a basal value similar to Wisconsins that influences prices up to MS64. In 65 and 66 a small premium develops; these are a good value for the collector as he/she is able to purchase a gem quality coin for near-basal money. In 67, Yorks take their first significant price jump. The high population may not support this level in the future and purchases of MS67 coins should be considered carefully.

- ✓ At current price levels, do not purchase below grade 65.
- ✓ Yorks are readily available untoned up to 66. Expect 67 coins to have some toning.
- ✓ Avoid coins with significant or multiple hits on the obverse shield area.
- ✓ Author's choice: *Collector* MS65; *Investor* MS66. This issue is Recommended.

Chapter 4

THE GOLD COMMEMORATIVES

$1 Jefferson
1903

Mintage
Business strikes: 17,500
Ranking: (10)

Certified Populations & Historical Values

	MS60	MS62	MS63	MS64	MS65	MS66	MS67
Pop.	17	192	450	694	441	115	13
Rank	(7)	(6)	(10)	(10)	(11)	(11)	(11)
Pricing							
1957	—	—	$ 32	—	—	—	—
1970	—	—	90	—	—	—	—
1980	$ 650	—	875	—	$ 1,275	—	—
1982	500	—	850	—	1,300	$ 2,275	—
1989	650	$ 1,125	2,300	$ 3,900	7,625	14,500	$45,000
1994	330	575	1,070	1,650	2,370	4,120	13,500

Percent of mintage certified..11%
Popular collector grades.................................MS60-64   Popular investor grades...................................MS64-67
Background: Louisiana Purchase Exposition in St. Louis, 1904

Comments

The Louisiana Purchase Jefferson and its sister coin, the McKinley, have the highest mintages of the 13-piece gold commemorative set with the exception of the $2.50 Sesqui. The Jefferson's certified rankings nearly mimic its mintage rankings as all grades from MS63 on rank either 10th or 11th. Prices are way down from 1989 highs, with grades 65 through 67 showing the largest percentage decreases.

The Jefferson is often seen with a hard frosty luster. Some die polishing may also be evident. These coins are tiny in comparison to commemorative halves but still manage to pick up hairlines. Luster impairment is another problem for Jeffersons as well as for all other gold commemoratives. It is usually caused by mishandling, poor storage or improper cleaning.

Price increases from grade to grade are steady, with the only multiple jump occurring between MS66 and 67. Collectors are primarily interested in grades 64 and below. Grades 60 to 62 are well supported and these lower-grade examples find homes quickly. MS63 and MS64 grades are being aggressively marketed in sets and many coins have been taken off the market. MS65's have a relatively small premium over 64's, making them attractively priced for the investor. MS66 and MS67 specimens are fully priced and purchases of 67's should be considered speculative.

- ✓ Avoid coins with significant scratches or bag marks. These coins are too small to allow much damage.
- ✓ Coins with copper spots or copper toning may currently trade at discounts.
- ✓ Slightly more common than its sister coin the McKinley.
- ✓ Author's choice: *Collector* MS63; *Investor* MS65. This issue is Recommended.

$1 McKinley
1903

Mintage
Business strikes: 17,500
Ranking: (10)

Certified Populations & Historical Values

	MS60	MS62	MS63	MS64	MS65	MS66	MS67
Pop.	39	267	432	529	338	129	9
Rank	(9)	(10)	(9)	(7)	(8)	(12)	(10)
Pricing							
1957	—	—	$ 35	—	—	—	—
1970	—	—	90	—	—	—	—
1980	$ 650	—	875	—	$ 1,275	—	—
1982	500	—	850	—	1,300	$ 2,275	—
1989	650	$ 950	2,150	$ 3,650	8,225	16,040	$45,000
1994	320	525	1,020	1,670	2,400	4,000	15,000

Percent of mintage certified..10%
Popular collector grades.................................MS60-64   Popular investor grades................................MS64-67
Background: Louisiana Purchase Exposition in St. Louis, 1904

Comments

The McKinley is the second Louisiana Purchase gold dollar, with an identical mintage to the Jefferson. The McKinley's population rankings are higher overall and, specifically in grades MS63 through 65 and 67. MS65 and 66 graded coins have declined by the largest percentage. Like the Jefferson, the McKinley's luster is strong and sometimes appears almost caked on. This issue can suffer from severe die polishing which can easily cost the coin a grade. Die cracks and bubbly surfaces may exist on the reverse.

Prices for the McKinley are almost identical to the Jefferson in grades up to 65. These coins are purchased by set builders, with most activity centering on 63 to 65. These grades are appropriately priced and nice specimens move off the market quickly. MS66 and 67 coins are supported solely by investors and both should be considered somewhat speculative, with MS67 having the greatest risk.

✓ Avoid coins with large defects and copper spots.
✓ Currently in demand due to large, long-term promotions.
✓ Die polishing may be a factor in eye appeal.
✓ Author's choice: *Collector* MS63; *Investor* MS65. This issue is Recommended.

Harry Laibstain

$1 Lewis & Clark
1904

Mintage
Business strikes: 10,025
Ranking: (8)

Certified Populations & Historical Values

	MS60	MS62	MS63	MS64	MS65	MS66	MS67
Pop.	22	202	301	339	152	44	5
Rank	(8)	(7)	(6)	(4)	(5)	(5)	(7)
Pricing							
1957	—	—	$ 140	—	—	—	—
1970	—	—	360	—	—	—	—
1980	$ 1,750	—	2,400	—	$ 3,600	—	—
1982	1,000	—	1,750	—	3,000	$ 4,750	—
1989	1,050	$ 1,840	5,025	$ 3,650	22,225	41,100	$85,000
1994	660	1,100	2,420	3,800	5,150	7,550	23,000

Percent of mintage certified..11%
Popular collector grades..............................MS60-64   Popular investor grades...................................MS64-66
Background: The 100th anniversary of the Lewis and Clark expedition

Comments

With a mintage ranking of 8, the 1904 Lewis and Clark belies its own rarity. It has an average population ranking of 5 in the most important grades – MS63 to 66. This issue has suffered significant losses since 1989, particularly in grades 65 and above. The population peaks in grade 64 with a strong lean to 63. The coins are well spread across the range and, despite price declines, significant price jumps still exist between grades. Lewis and Clark gold dollars are the most likely issues to have quality problems because they really have two delicate obverse-style designs without the typical reverse (whose designs are generally protected). To make matters worse, they have exposed fields and flat open devices that show hairlines. Although specimens with intense luster are available, finding them without hairlines is very difficult.

In early 1989 I was fortunate to purchase (with partners) a commem gold set that had smooth-looking Lewis and Clarks. Both coins were coated with PVC and unidentifiable grime. I expected these coins to brighten up and was particularly pleased when I discovered they were virtually hairline free. Both coins graded 65 and were sold at the peak of the market during the ANA mid-year convention in San Diego (1989).

1904 Lewis and Clarks have taken a beating since that time. Grades 64 and below have managed to hold on to at least 50% of their value and seem reasonably priced, but higher grades have not fared as well. MS65 specimens that sold in the $20,000 range are worth a quarter of that today. MS66 coins have done even worse, losing over 80% of their value. Two phenomenons fueled those high prices in 1989. First, populations were low and values could be manipulated. Second, a California dealer with deep pockets was pressing the price levels higher and higher. Eventually his strategy backfired and he later sold many coins at substantial losses. Since then, price spreads for this issue have grown tighter and make more sense. Both 65's and 66's have moderate spreads from their proceeding grades and growth potential is once again possible. MS67 specimens should be considered somewhat speculative even though they trade around the 1989 MS65 price.

- ✓ Not as rare as the 1905 but still one of the keys to the 11 piece set.
- ✓ Look for coins with strong luster. Avoid any deep cuts or spotting.
- ✓ Do not expect market highs to be reached again. However, dramatic price decreases leave this coin with plenty of room for growth.
- ✓ Author's choice: *Collector* MS63; *Investor* MS65. This issue is Highly Recommended.

$1 Lewis & Clark
1905

Mintage
Business strikes: 10,041
Ranking: (9)

Certified Populations & Historical Values

	MS60	MS62	MS63	MS64	MS65	MS66	MS67
Pop.	41	203	274	229	74	6	0
Rank	(11)	(8)	(4)	(3)	(3)	(4)	(1)
Pricing							
1957	—	—	$ 130	—	—	—	—
1970	—	—	370	—	—	—	—
1980	$ 1,750	—	2,400	—	$ 3,600	—	—
1982	1,000	—	1,750	—	3,000	$ 4,750	—
1989	1,050	$ 2,250	5,650	$11,100	32,100	75,000	$100,000
1994	750	1,575	3,000	5,100	13,500	34,000	60,000

Percent of mintage certified..9%
Popular collector grades..MS60-64 Popular investor grades..MS64-66
Background: The 100th anniversary of the Lewis and Clark expedition

Comments

The 1905 Lewis and Clark, like the 1904, ranks low in mintage (9th of 13) in contrast to its actual rarity. In grades 63 to 66 its population ranking averages just 3.5, making it the rarest issue excluding the $50 pieces. Although price declines have been substantial, the percentage decrease is less than many other gold issues including the 1904. 1905 Lewis and Clarks suffer from the same quality problems as the 1904 – two obverse designs and a predisposition to hairlines cause these coins to grade low. Add to that the low percentage certified (9%) and a population that peaks in 63, and you begin to understand the difficulty in locating high-grade specimens. Gold commems are most often collected as an a 11-piece set, leaving out the two gold $50 pieces. The 1905 Lewis and Clark is the key of the 11 and will continue to enjoy strong demand from set builders and hoarders.

Prices in the lower grades have not declined by much and coins graded 62 and below are in demand from price buyers and raw coin dealers. When available, these sell quickly. MS63 and 64 coins are strongly supported by set builders; spot-free, properly graded examples sell immediately. Due to large price spreads, many of these are resubmitted in the hopes of attaining a higher grade and a big payoff. I do not recommend this for inexperienced coin graders because coins that are resubmitted may also grade lower. MS65 specimens, which are still expensive, probably represent good value as competition for this very scarce coin continues to keep pressure on prices. In 1989, MS65 specimens reached $40,000 wholesale and I registered several sales to dealers around that level. One specimen even brought $48,000 in a group but was later sold back at a pre arranged "buy back" of $44,000. It was then resold again at $44,000. Don't expect to see these levels anytime soon. The current era cannot be compared to the circumstances of 1989 when populations were low and one major player was having a strong influence over commem gold prices. However, I certainly see potential for growth among those issues and grades most heavily demanded within a set.

✓ Look for coins with good luster and no copper spots.
✓ Key to 11-piece set. Subject to hoarding; also has set-building demand.
✓ Do not expect market highs to be reached again; however, excellent growth potential exists at current levels.
✓ Author's choice: *Collector* MS63; *Investor* MS65. This issue is Highly Recommended.

Harry Laibstain

$1 Panama-Pacific
1915-S

Mintage
Business strikes: 15,000
Ranking: (12)

Certified Populations & Historical Values

	MS60	MS62	MS63	MS64	MS65	MS66	MS67
Pop.	39	393	872	940	528	112	5
Rank	(9)	(12)	(12)	(12)	(13)	(10)	(7)
Pricing							
1957	—	—	$ 19	—	—	—	—
1970	—	—	72	—	—	—	—
1980	$ 825	—	1,275	—	$ 2,750	—	—
1982	975	—	975	—	1,675	$ 2,950	—
1989	600	$ 1,175	1,950	$ 3,600	7,950	27,000	$71,000
1994	340	525	970	1,550	2,150	4,220	20,000

Percent of mintage certified..20%
Popular collector grades................................MS60-64   Popular investor grades................................MS64-67
Background: Panama-Pacific International Exposition

Comments

The Panama-Pacific gold dollar is the most common of the four gold commemoratives from the Pan-Pac set. With a mintage of 15,000 it ranks just ahead of the two Louisiana Purchase dollars and the $2.50 Sesqui. Its population rankings are very low and it is the most common commemorative gold issue in MS65. Additionally, it is second most common in the important middle grades from 62 to 64.

Pan-Pacs come with a nice frosty luster. Occasionally Pan-Pac dollars will suffer from struck-throughs or other die imperfections. These may affect grade but are more likely to influence eye appeal. Pan-Pacs are one of the few coins in either the gold or silver commemorative sets that seem to be allowed to have rub and still grade up to 63. Up to this grade, the laborer's baseball cap will usually show some luster friction. Compare the skin on the cap of a lower grade coin to a really choice specimen and this will be evident.

Prices for Pan-Pac dollars follow a consistent trend and compare closely, although slightly lower, to the Louisiana Purchase issues. Grades 63 to 65 are strongly supported by set builders and current prices are accurate. MS66 coins have decreased by almost 85% since 1989, giving them the largest percentage decline of any gold commem. This is misleading as populations were considerably lower on commemorative gold in the late 1980's, particularly for MS66's. I recall selling several pieces at that time for around $20,000 each when the population was approximately 25. MS67 specimens are very rare and expensive. Purchase at this time should be considered speculative even though the price has declined by $51,000!

- ✓ Most common commemorative gold dollar in grades to 65.
- ✓ Population increases have greatly influenced prices.
- ✓ Try to purchase examples in middle grades with full luster on the cap.
- ✓ Author's choice: *Collector* MS64; *Investor* MS65. This issue is Recommended.

$2.50 Panama-Pacific
1915-S

Mintage
Business strikes: 6,749
Ranking: (5)

Certified Populations & Historical Values

	MS60	MS62	MS63	MS64	MS65	MS66	MS67
Pop.	9	129	305	564	430	77	8
Rank	(2)	(5)	(7)	(9)	(10)	(7)	(9)
Pricing							
1957	—	—	$ 95	—	—	—	—
1970	—	—	328	—	—	—	—
1980	$ 2,650	—	3,750	—	$ 6,650	—	—
1982	2,100	—	2,150	—	5,000	$ 7,500	—
1989	1,500	$ 2,650	4,425	$ 6,900	11,500	27,100	$65,000
1994	1,100	1,625	2,310	3,120	4,060	6,500	16,500

Percent of mintage certified..23%
Popular collector grades.................................MS60-64   Popular investor grades..................................MS64-67
Background: Panama-Pacific International Exposition

Comments

The $2.50 Pan-Pac commemorative ranks high in mintage and moderate-to-low in certified population. With an average ranking of nearly 9th between grades 64 and 67, this issue prices above coins that are scarcer. Perhaps this can be explained by its higher face value and larger size. In addition, demand based on low mintage may be a factor.

$2.50 Pan-Pacs have a frosty luster that can be very intense. The coins also have circular and multi-directional die polishing. This does not usually distract from their grade or appearance as virtually all specimens display this characteristic. Its surfaces remind me of the Spanish Trail, where light die polish is also an ever present part of the issue. Many Pan-Pacs that have been lightly cleaned still qualify for some mint state grade. The grade this coin receives often depends on how fresh and original the surfaces are.

$2.50 Pan-Pacs have a high basal value, which may be another reason why their prices are higher than scarcer coins in the same series. Coins below 63 are virtually unavailable. They sell quickly to collectors on a budget and raw-coin dealers who can crack them out and market them to non-certified buyers. MS63 and 64 coins are generally the least expensive examples available and sell quickly. MS65's and 66's are a little overpriced in relation to their population and tend to sell a little slower. However, the longer the current promotion of these issues goes on, the better commemorative gold will do. As these coins go off the market, availability will decrease and prices should escalate.

✓ Low-mintage, high-population issue probably overrated in technical terms.
✓ Expect some weakness of strike which is typical of this issue.
✓ Avoid dull, lackluster examples of this coin; they have probably been lightly cleaned.
✓ Author's choice: *Collector* MS64; *Investor* MS65. This issue is Recommended.

TIPS!

Harry Laibstain

$50 Round Panama-Pacific
1915-S

Mintage
Business strikes: 483
Ranking: (1)

Certified Populations & Historical Values

	MS60	MS62	MS63	MS64	MS65	MS66	MS67
Pop.	7	40	61	54	9	3	0
Rank	(1)	(1)	(1)	(2)	(2)	(2)	(1)
Pricing							
1957	—	—	$ 1,800	—	—	—	—
1970	—	—	6,000	—	—	—	—
1980	$ 16,000	—	16,750	—	$18,000	—	—
1982	24,000	—	27,500	—	32,000	$42,500	—
1989	35,000	$52,500	63,000	$89,000	130,000	275,000	$375,000
1994	20,000	24,000	30,000	38,000	85,000	125,000	175,000

Percent of mintage certified............41%
Popular collector grades............AU58-MS63   Popular investor grades............MS63-65
Background: Panama-Pacific International Exposition

Comments

The Panama-Pacific $50 round is the lowest mintage commemorative ever coined. Just over 40% of the rounds have been graded, perhaps 10% of them regrades. (PCGS adjusts their population figures and NGC does not.) That leaves something less than 200 coins that have not been sent in or are unsuitable for certification. Although fewer in total mint state (198 versus 253), rounds apparently were either preserved better or are a higher quality issue than octagons. The population peaks a full grade higher in MS63 and the lean is toward 64. MS64 rounds are 50% more common than octagons of the same grade and a similar relationships exists among coins that grade 65 and above. As noted before, this has not caused the price trend to change and rounds price higher than octagons in every grade. Nevertheless, rounds were prone to some mishandling and this accounts for the shortage of gem specimens. A gold coin of this size and weight picks up hairlines and nicks easily.

This coin takes reasonable price jumps in grades up to 64 and then advances almost $50,000 from 64 to 65. Coins that grade 62 to 64 appear to represent the best value and should be available based on population data. Expect to pay a premium for nice examples. This coin is truly rare and seldom sells for bid. Purchase of 65 or 66 specimens should be considered speculative as these thinly traded issues may not be subject to the natural laws of supply and demand as their lower grade counterparts.

- ✓ Avoid cleaned, damaged or repaired specimens.
- ✓ 65 and 66 prices are the only grades that have appreciated greatly over the 1980-1982 market.
- ✓ Prices for grades 64 and below have bottomed out, however, purchase of this coin in any grade involves risk.
- ✓ Author's choice: *Collector* MS62; *Investor* MS64. This issue is Recommended.

$50 Octagonal Panama-Pacific
1915-S

Mintage
Business strikes: 645
Ranking: (2)

Certified Populations & Historical Values

	MS60	MS62	MS63	MS64	MS65	MS66	MS67
Pop.	14	84	77	35	8	0	0
Rank	(6)	(3)	(2)	(1)	(1)	(1)	(1)
Pricing							
1957	—	—	$ 1,550	—	—	—	—
1970	—	—	4,750	—	—	—	—
1980	$ 13,000	—	13,500	—	$15,000	—	—
1982	16,500	—	19,000	—	23,000	$31,000	—
1989	26,000	$42,000	47,500	$89,000	125,000	260,000	$360,000
1994	18,000	21,000	25,000	34,000	75,000	100,000	140,000

Percent of mintage certified..39%
Popular collector grades ....AU58-MS63 Popular investor grades..MS63-65
Background: Panama-Pacific International Exposition

Comments

The Panama-Pacific $50 octagonal is the only eight-sided commemorative coin ever minted by the U.S. Its mintage is slightly higher than the round $50 piece because its distinctive shape helped it sell better. Although more common overall, the octagonal is scarcer than the round in grades 64 and higher. Curiously, this does not reflect in the values as rounds outprice octagons in every grade. Population is concentrated in the lower grades, the peak coming in MS62, with a strong lean toward 63. Large as these coins are, they are subject to much mishandling. Many specimens have been improperly cleaned and suffer from impaired luster or hairlining problems. Gem-quality coins are almost nonexistent. This is actually a little surprising since many were preserved in presentation sets.

These large gold coins are expensive and are only for the advanced collector or investor with deep pockets. Decent specimens cannot be purchased for less than $20,000 and you should expect to pay mid to upper $20,000's for almost any certified mint-state coin. Price declines have been significant since 1989 but current levels are still well above those of the early 1980's. Perhaps the most significant declines have been in MS63 and 64. Prices seem reasonable now and populations indicate that coins should be on the market, at least occasionally. Proceed with caution when purchasing this coin. Prices have remained stable for several years and many dealers feel these coins have bottomed out. However, coins that sell for these lofty prices automatically have downside risk.

- ✓ Octagons are more common overall but scarcer than $50 rounds in high grades.
- ✓ Avoid cleaned, damaged or repaired specimens.
- ✓ Check your finances before purchasing either of the Pan-Pac $50 coins. In 64 either one will cost you as much as a complete 144-piece set of the silver commemoratives.
- ✓ Author's choice: *Collector* MS62; *Investor* MS64. This issue is Recommended.

Harry Laibstain

$1 McKinley
1916

Mintage
Business strikes: 9,977
Ranking: (6)

Certified Populations & Historical Values

	MS60	MS62	MS63	MS64	MS65	MS66	MS67
Pop.	44	361	675	814	358	105	4
Rank	(12)	(11)	(11)	(11)	(9)	(8)	(6)
Pricing							
1957	—	—	$ 25	—	—	—	—
1970	—	—	82	—	—	—	—
1980	$ 680	—	825	—	$ 1,250	—	—
1982	800	—	800	—	1,450	$ 2,500	—
1989	650	$ 1,025	1,875	$ 3,125	8,725	18,200	$60,000
1994	350	520	910	1,280	2,250	4,400	18,000

Percent of mintage certified 25%
Popular collector grades .... MS60-64 Popular investor grades MS64-67
Background: To commemorate President McKinley and help pay for a memorial building at his birthplace

Comments

The 1916 McKinley has a slightly lower mintage than its sister coin, the 1917, but it is the more common of this two-year issue. Even though the mintage is relatively low, certified populations are high – particularly in grades 64 and below. In MS65 and 66 the 1916 manages to edge out a few competitors and establish a modicum of rarity. This issue's rarity closely aligns with the $1 Pan-Pac, yet its prices in grades to 64 appear lower. Additionally, its 65 price is lower than several issues whose populations are greater.

The 1916 McKinley comes with strong luster and is sometimes found in varying degrees of proof-like. The obverse is most likely to have problems, when there are any, as the reverse is almost always gem. Obverse problems include hairlines or cuts in the open fields and cuts or light scratches in the face and hair of McKinley. Demand for 1916 McKinley's is similar to other issues in the series. Strong collector/investor demand continues to pursue these issues. Many coins are currently off the market. Prices in 64 and 65 could currently support levels that are 10% higher, which would bring them in line with the price-population ratios of other gold commems.

- ✓ Coins with copper spots currently trade at discounts.
- ✓ Grade this coin primarily by the obverse.
- ✓ Available in proof-like but does not command a premium.
- ✓ Author's choice: *Collector* <u>MS64</u>; *Investor* <u>MS65</u>. This issue is <u>Recommended</u>.

$1 McKinley
1917

Mintage
Business strikes: 10,000
Ranking: (7)

Certified Populations & Historical Values

	MS60	MS62	MS63	MS64	MS65	MS66	MS67
Pop.	11	218	420	508	212	66	3
Rank	(4)	(9)	(8)	(6)	(6)	(6)	(5)
Pricing							
1957	—	—	$ 28	—	—	—	—
1970	—	—	135	—	—	—	—
1980	$ 725	—	925	—	$ 1,350	—	—
1982	575	—	875	—	1,700	$ 3,000	—
1989	675	$ 1,150	2,275	$ 4,050	9,100	26,100	$60,000
1994	390	775	1,230	1,910	3,080	5,850	25,000

Percent of mintage certified............15%
Popular collector grades............MS60-64   Popular investor grades............MS64-67
Background: To commemorate President McKinley and help pay for a memorial building at his birthplace

Comments

The 1917 McKinley is the scarcer of this two-year issue. Its mintage of 10,000 puts it right in the middle of the gold commem series, with six issues under and six issues over. In grades 64 and higher it outperforms its mintage ranking, achieving an average of just under 6th. The 1917 McKinley has the same design as the 1916 and its characteristics are similar. One difference is the higher number of ungradeable examples in the 1917's. This is demonstrated by the difference in percent certified between the two issues (25% versus 15%).

1917 McKinleys sell quickly in all grades below 63, as price shoppers and raw-coin dealers scoop up the available supply. The population of this coin peaks in 64 with a strong lean toward 63. MS63 and 64 coins are being actively pursued by investors and collectors. If we exclude the $50 pieces which are in a class of their own, only three issues are scarcer in the 64 to 66 range. In 64 one of these (Grant) becomes more common in high grades. In 65 and 66 only the Lewis and Clarks and the 1925 Sesqui are scarcer.

The 1917 is a pivotal coin, nestled just above the common issues and just below the scarcer issues. Its prices are more in line with the lower ranking issues and this makes it one of the series' best values.

- ✓ Good value across the grade range. Good growth potential.
- ✓ Grade this issue primarily by the obverse. Avoid deep cuts, long scratches or copper spots.
- ✓ Counterfeits do exist. Purchase this coin (as well as any gold commem) certified.
- ✓ Author's choice: *Collector* MS64; *Investor* MS65. This issue is <u>Highly Recommended</u>.

Harry Laibstain

$1 Grant
1922

Mintage
Business strikes: 5,000
Ranking: (3)

Certified Populations & Historical Values

	MS60	MS62	MS63	MS64	MS65	MS66	MS67
Pop.	10	106	296	438	289	111	16
Rank	(3)	(4)	(5)	(5)	(7)	(9)	(12)
Pricing							
1957	—	—	$ 85	—	—	—	—
1970	—	—	300	—	—	—	—
1980	$ 1,425	—	1,850	—	$ 2,850	—	—
1982	800	—	1,300	—	2,000	$ 3,500	—
1989	1,800	$ 2,750	3,925	$ 5,350	8,700	17,750	$65,000
1994	1,000	1,350	1,670	2,020	2,580	3,900	10,000

Percent of mintage certified..26%
Popular collector grades..MS60-64 Popular investor grades..MS64-67
Background: The 100th anniversary of Ulysses S. Grant's birth

Comments

The Grant gold dollar is part of a four-coin set that also includes a Grant/Star gold dollar and two silver half-dollar issues. Unlike the half dollars, the gold dollars have similar (low) mintages. This issue ranks 3rd in mintage but lower in certified grades from 62 on. Although scarce by mintage standards, Grants were obviously saved and well preserved. Population rankings decline in every grade until 67, where it is the most common issue with the exception of its sister coin, the Grant/Star. Price jumps between grades are moderate, as is often the case with high-quality issues. Grants usually come nice with a strong thick luster. The design is busy and the only open areas are the small obverse fields. The reverse is usually gem with any problems likely to involve impaired luster.

Grant dollars are virtually unavailable in low grades. Due to the high quality of this issue and its low mintage the coin enjoys a very high basal value. Dealers trying to purchase a decent specimen are often forced to go as high as MS63 to fill their order. With coins graded 63 and lower enjoying demand from several directions, they are quite difficult to locate. MS64 and 65 specimens take moderate price jumps and represent good value for the collector. Their rankings in these grades are actually quite high but some allowance must be made because of availability in higher grades. MS66 coins are reasonably priced as they have experienced massive declines since 1989. MS67 examples are still rather expensive as their current low populations could increase in the future, diluting values even further.

✓ Grant dollars are popular because of their low mintages.
✓ Do not purchase this coin below grade 63.
✓ Expect these to be nice. Full luster and a lack of bag marks is the norm for this issue in grades 64 and above.
✓ Author's choice: *Collector* MS64; *Investor* MS66.

TIPS!

$1 Grant/Star
1922

Mintage
Business strikes: 5,016
Ranking: (4)

Certified Populations & Historical Values

	MS60	MS62	MS63	MS64	MS65	MS66	MS67
Pop.	12	52	235	541	456	175	33
Rank	(5)	(2)	(3)	(8)	(12)	(13)	(13)
Pricing							
1957	—	—	$ 70	—	—	—	—
1970	—	—	285	—	—	—	—
1980	$ 1,425	—	1,850	—	$ 2,850	—	—
1982	800	—	1,300	—	2,000	$ 3,500	—
1989	1,950	$ 2,950	4,250	$ 5,475	8,625	14,700	$35,500
1994	1,150	1,525	1,650	2,030	2,700	3,500	8,500

Percent of mintage certified..30%
Popular collector grades..............................MS60-64   Popular investor grades..MS64-67
Background: The 100th anniversary of Ulysses S. Grant's birth

Comments

The Grant/Star gold dollar is similar in mintage and combined rarity to its sister coin, the no-star. The most obvious difference occurs in grade rarities from MS64 on. The Grant/Star is the highest quality issue of the entire gold set. In 66 and 67 it is the most common issue and in 65 it is second most common, edged out by the Pan-Pac dollar. Although the population peaks in grade 64, there is a very strong lean to 65 while 66 specimens are almost as common as 63's.

Grant/Star dollars were produced first. The star was later removed to complete production, which partially explains why the with-stars are nicer than the no-stars. Having come from the earlier strikes, this issue is found with thick, frosty luster and does not have as many marks as other issues. The texture of the surfaces and thickness of mint luster seem to protect them somewhat from hairlining problems.

Pricing on the Grant/Star is similar to the no-star. In grades below 64 this issue is supported by demand from the bottom up where any decent example will fill the order. Dealers who pursue these lower-grade coins are usually thrilled to find an MS60 which they can market at the same price they would a 63. These low-grade specimens are even more difficult to locate than the no-stars because most of the population is concentrated in grades 64 and above. Both Grants sell for similar prices in 65 and 66, which is surprising. The no-star is a better value at similar levels due to significantly lower populations. There is obviously some excess demand for the with-star variety that keeps these levels even. MS67 takes a large jump from 66 price and most would be hard pressed to discern the actual difference in quality between these two grades. At $5,000 more than the 66, MS67 coins seem expensive.

- ✓ Do not purchase this coin below 63 and expect it to have good eye appeal. Avoid dull luster or copper spots.
- ✓ Grant/Stars have similar pricing to no-stars but populations are significantly higher.
- ✓ Most common commem gold issue in better grades. Underperforms its attractive low mintage.
- ✓ Author's choice: *Collector* MS64; *Investor* MS66.

Harry Laibstain

$2.50 Sesquicentennial
1926

Mintage
Business strikes: 46,019
Ranking: (13)

Certified Populations & Historical Values

	MS60	MS62	MS63	MS64	MS65	MS66	MS67
Pop.	132	1,217	1,659	1,219	149	5	0
Rank	(13)	(13)	(13)	(13)	(4)	(3)	(1)
Pricing							
1957	—	—	$ 20	—	—	—	—
1970	—	—	62	—	—	—	—
1980	$ 490	—	650	—	$ 850	—	—
1982	460	—	675	—	1,100	$ 1,950	—
1989	500	$ 850	1,450	$ 3,725	23,700	60,000	$100,000
1994	275	380	705	1,270	6,650	32,000	65,000

Percent of mintage certified...10%
Popular collector grades.................................MS60-64 Popular investor grades.................................MS64-65
Background: 150th anniversary of the signing of the Declaration of Independence

Comments

The 1926 Sesquicentennial was the second and final $2.50 commemorative issued and is part of a two-coin set that includes a Sesqui half dollar of the same date. Both coins share an interesting trait. Although the mintages were high and the coins widely dispersed, gem quality specimens MS65 and greater are very rare. The $2.50 Sesqui is a prime example of grade rarity. In grades 64 and below it is the most common gold commemorative in the series, ranking 13th in every grade. High mintage is responsible for these rankings as opposed to production quality or design. The sheer number of coins certified, almost 5,000, fill up these grades. In MS65, the ranking increases 9 points and is edged out only by the 1905 Lewis and Clark and the two $50 gold pieces.

Prices that form a consistent pattern in the lower grades take a huge leap from 64 to 65. Unlike the lower grades, MS65 specimens are not influenced by mintage. Design becomes the determining factor in this grade. Sesqui $2.50's have exposed fields, obverse and reverse. In addition, the devices on both sides are flat and lack detail. This coin's surfaces act like a magnet to ticks, cuts and hairlines. It is not unusual to see reed marks from the edge of another coin in the surface. Finding specimens with the right combination of luster, originality and lack of bag marks sufficient to grade 65 is a difficult task.

Sesquis are relatively inexpensive in grades 60 to 64. They are often compared in promotions to the $2.50 Indians that were minted between 1908 and 1929. As a group, $2.50 Indians are more common than the Sesqui, yet Sesquis trade for less. This may be an unfair comparison of a one-year type coin to an entire set. Either demand will pick up on this issue and prices will increase or populations have grown too large for real growth potential. This is a tough call but I'm inclined to go with the latter.

In MS65, declines have cost some investors as much as 70%. Even though demand is high for MS65 gold commemoratives, both collectors and (to a lesser extent) investors will resist paying a 500% premium for one more grade point. Currently the market seems able to absorb all MS65 Sesquis that are available but the large spread between 64 and 65 will insure lots of energy and money are spent trying to upgrade this issue. If this happens, new production could glut the market and cause prices to slip further. MS66 coins are expensive and highly speculative. Reported prices on these thinly traded issues may be inaccurate.

✓ Excellent example of grade rarity.
✓ MS64 population may be over inflated due to the number of regrades.
✓ Less expensive as a type coin than the more common $2.50 Indians from the same period in MS64 and below.
✓ Author's choice: *Collector* MS63; *Investor* MS64.

Chapter 5

PROOF-LIKE COMMEMORATIVES

PROOF-LIKE COMMEMORATIVES

By Yitzy Gedalowitz

A small number of certified commems have been designated as Proof-like (P/L) on their holders by NGC (PCGS does not denote this for commems). These are listed in *Table 11*. As you can see, 27 of the 144 silver issues have P/L examples and, of these, only nine have had more than ten pieces graded to date. Three issues – 1892 and 1893 Columbian Expositions and New Rochelle – have had more P/L's certified than all others combined. Obviously, most P/L commems are very scarce.

P/L commems range from coins with moderate mirror surfaces, often deeper on the obverse, to pieces with deep-mirror surfaces on both sides. However, unlike Morgan Dollars where PL and DMPL designations are used, the degree of proof-likeness is not differentiated on commemorative holders. They are all simply designated as PL. These coins generally bring a premium of from 50 to more than 200% over their non P/L counterparts, depending on several factors including the value of the equivalent non-P/L coin and the actual appearance of the coin itself. Inexpensive issues like the 1947-S and 1950-S BTW's bring approximately $125 in MS65 condition vs only $40 - $50 in non P/L. These carry the greatest premiums on a percentage basis. The highest premiums for a given issue tend to be for coins which have grade rarity. The following is a discussion of P/L commem characteristics and variations for each issue graded, and for some issues which have not yet been graded but may be found in proof-like condition.

Isabella quarters can be located with deep P/L surfaces. In fact, before the advent of the grading services, P/L Isabellas were often sold as proofs. Today 26 Isabellas have been graded P/L, 24 of which are in MS64 and below. Only one each has been graded in MS65 and MS66. Proof-like Isabellas sell for approximately a 50% premium for nicely toned examples, with white cameos going for 100 - 125% over their non P/L counterparts. Any new coin graded above MS65 would likely bring a substantial premium because of its rarity.

The Boone series contains a number of issues which come in P/L condition, but only the 1937-S with 48 coins graded is readily available. This issue can often be found with deep P/L surfaces and many have some degree of reflectivity. The only P and D Mint Boones that come with any degree of reflectivity are the '37-P and D. They often have P/L surfaces on the obverse, but satiny reverses. This lack of mirror surfaces on the reverse explains why so few have been graded as P/L. A few '38-S Boones can be found in MS63 and 64, but only one has been graded higher. This issue does not come with the same depth as the '37-S. A single '36-S has been graded to date (in 64) and no 35-S Boones have been graded. However, it's likely that a '35-s may exist.

To date, only a single '36-P Cincinnati has been graded. This issue does come with shallow P/L surfaces and thus others should exist. No '36-D Cincinnati has been graded, but it comes like the '36-P and some may be graded in the future. As far as I know, '36-S Cincinnatis do not come in P/L condition.

1892 and 1893 Columbians are among the most common P/L commems and they often come with deep P/L surfaces. The '93 is scarcer than the '92 in all grades and is particularly rare above MS65. Expect to pay at least 100% premium for lower grades, while higher grades will trade between 50 and 100% over non-P/L examples.

Delawares also come in P/L condition, but the mirror is usually not deep. Just 5 have been graded in 64 with 3 higher. Being scarce, these command a strong premium (in the 150 to 200% range).

New Rochelle is the second most common commem in P/L condition with a total of 101 graded. They often come with deep P/L surfaces and there is some question whether or not these actually are proofs. However, the grading services believe that proofs do not exist for this issue. (In some cases hand-written letters from Walter Breen proclaiming that he believed they were proofs are available). Expect to pay approximately $450, $700 and $1,250 for this issue in MS64, 65 and 66 respectively.

Roanokes are also relatively common P/L issues, with 26 graded to date. Of these, 17 are MS65 and only two are higher grades. The P/L's of this issue range from deep proof-like surfaces to surfaces which are just proof-like. Expect to pay $450 - $500 for an MS65.

Eight of the BTW issues come with P/L surfaces; the '47-S and '50-S account for the majority of these. Both often come in deep proof-like condition. The other five which have P/L representatives usually do not come with deep mirror surfaces. Although no '47-P BTW has been graded I have seen them and some may be graded in the future. Expect to pay around $125 - $150 in MS65 for the more common BTW's and $250 - $300 for the '48-S, '49-P and '51-S in MS65. The '46-S with a pop of just two in MS65 is probably worth $400 to the specialist and the '48-P and '51-D (pop of one each) could bring between $750 and $1,000.

Washington-Carvers can be found in P/L condition but, except for the '52-D, they are rare. The '51-P and '52-S have also had some examples graded. In addition, the following issues exist in P/L condition, although none have been graded to date: '51-D, '53-P and D, '54-P, D and S. None of the W-C issues come with deep mirrors.

Eight of the '37-S Texas have been graded P/L, however they often come with shallow reverses. If these same standards are applied to a '38-S in the future it too should have some proof-like examples. In the market the scarcity of P/L coins of this type is weighed against the lack of depth of the mirror surfaces. Expect to pay approximately $300 - $400 for an MS65.

The '36-P Rhode Island is fairly common in P/L condition and often comes with deep mirrors. A total of 31 have been graded. These are extremely scarce above MS65. There have been two '36-S Rhode Islands graded P/L in lower grades. This issue does not come with deep surfaces. I have not seen a '36-D of this type that was P/L, so putting a PDS set together is not yet possible. The '36-P is worth about $200 in MS64 and $500 in MS65.

Four examples of the '35-S San Diego have been graded P/L. This issue does not come with a deep mirror. Expect to pay from $350 - $450 in MS65.

In addition to the issues mentioned above, I have seen the following issues in P/L condition. Some of these may be graded in the future: Elgin, Gettysburg, Lincoln and Maine. Also, the following commems have been seen in P/L condition on the obverse only and there remains a remote possibility that some may yet be graded as P/L coins: Bridgeport, California, Cleveland, Grant, Grant with star, Maryland and '36-D San Diego.

In general, P/L commems are very scarce coins and those with deep mirrors on both sides are particularly desirable. This is an area where "cherry picking" is still possible as coins with mirror fields can sometimes still be found in PCGS holders, where they are not designated. Proof-like coins represent yet one more facet of the complex world of commemoratives. Since, to some extent, prices for these are based on current levels of their non-P/L counterparts, most are very reasonable considering their scarcity.

Table 11: NGC POPULATIONS OF PROOF-LIKE COMMEMS

RANK	TYPE	AU	60	61	62	63	64	65	66	67	TOTAL
1	'36-S Boone	0	0	0	0	0	1	0	0	0	1
	'37-P Boone	0	0	0	0	0	0	1	0	0	1
	'36-P Cinci	0	0	0	0	0	1	0	0	0	1
	'48-P BTW	0	0	0	0	0	0	1	0	0	1
	'51-D BTW	0	0	0	0	0	0	1	0	0	1
	'51-P W/C	0	0	0	0	1	0	0	0	0	1
	'36-S Rh. Island	0	0	0	1	1	0	0	0	0	1
8	'52-S W/C	0	0	0	0	0	1	1	0	0	2
9	'37-D Boone	0	0	0	0	0	3	0	0	0	3
10	'35-S San Diego	0	0	0	0	0	0	4	0	0	4
11	'49-P BTW	0	0	0	0	0	1	5	0	0	6
12	'52-D W/C	0	0	0	0	1	5	1	0	0	7
13	'38-S Boone	0	0	0	0	3	4	1	0	0	8
	Delaware	0	0	0	0	0	5	2	1	0	8
	'37-S Texas	0	0	0	0	1	2	4	1	0	8
	'46-S BTW	0	0	0	0	0	6	2	0	0	8
17	'48-S BTW	0	0	0	0	0	3	6	0	0	9
	'51-S BTW	0	0	0	0	0	0	6	3	0	9
19	Isabella	0	1	0	2	9	12	1	1	0	26
	Roanoke	0	0	0	0	2	5	17	2	0	26
21	'50-S BTW	0	0	0	0	0	4	17	6	0	27
22	'36-P Rh. Island	0	0	0	0	4	9	16	2	0	31
23	'47-S BTW	0	0	0	0	3	12	17	2	0	34
24	'37-S Boone	0	0	0	0	2	21	17	6	2	48
25	'93 Columbian	0	1	3	18	24	33	13	1	0	93
26	New Rochelle	0	0	0	0	5	35	27	26	8	101
27	'92 Columbian	6	3	9	24	50	65	34	6	0	197

Notes on table 11: 1) PCGS does not recognize whether or not a coin is P/L on the holder, therefore they offer no population data on these coins; 2) The figures above are based on March 1994 "NGC Census" figures.

Appendices

GLOSSARY

STATISTICS & TABLES

REFERENCES

APPENDIX A

GLOSSARY

BASAL VALUE – the value of an undamaged coin of a given issue in the lowest grade that it can be found in abundance.

BLUE SHEET – The *Certified Coin Dealer Newsletter* (colored blue). Published by CDN Inc. of Torrance, CA. Monitors sight unseen values of the wholesale market.

CONDITION RARITY – Issues which get scarcer in relation to other commemoratives as the grade increases.

CRACK OUT – A coin which is broken out of a certified holder. It may be to resubmit for an upgrade, to place in an album or for any other reason.

CROSS OVER – A coin in one type of certified holder submitted to a different service to have it holdered at the same grade. For example, sending in an NGC holdered coin to PCGS under their "cross over" service.

GRAY SHEET – The *Coin Dealer Newsletter* (colored gray). Published weekly by CDN Inc. of Torrance, CA. Monitors sight-seen wholesale values.

HAIR LINES – Very light lines on the surface of a coin caused by light cleaning, mishandling or another surface sliding over the coin.

INCUSE – Detail which is beneath the surface of the coin as opposed to being in relief. For example, the star of the Grant With Star issue.

MULTI-YEAR ISSUES – Coins of the same type issued over several years. For example, all the Oregon Trail commemoratives.

NGC – Numismatic Guaranty Corporation. One of the two major third party certification services. Located in Parsippany, NJ.

PCGS – Professional Coin Grading Service. One of the two major third party certification services. Located in Newport Beach, CA.

PDS SET – Set of the same year and type of coins from the Philadelphia, Denver and San Francisco Mints. For example, the 1936 – P,D & S issues of the Arkansas Centennial.

PQ – Premium Quality. Coins which are high end for the grade.

PROOF-LIKE (P/L) – A coin surface which is mirror-like or reflective, similar to that of a proof coin.

RANKING(S) – Coins are ranked from scarce (#1) to common (#144). A high ranking indicates a scarce coin but this will have a low number. For example, the 1935/34-D Boone ranks first in mintage (#1) — that is, it has the lowest mintage of the series.

RED BOOK – A common name for "A Guide Book of United States Coins" by R.S. Yeoman. Western Publ. Co., Racine, WI.

REED MARKS – Marks on a coin made by the edge reeding of another coin.

SIGHT SEEN = SIGHT bids – bids placed on the electronic trading networks to buy coins of a specific certified service and grade at a set price providing they meet the bidder's approval after he sees the coin.

SIGHT UNSEEN – Bids placed on the electronic trading networks to buy coins of a specific grade and holder at a set price regardless of their appearance.

STRUCK THROUGH – Coin which shows a mark or damage as a result of a foreign substance coming between the planchet and the die during production. The coin is said to have been struck through this material.

TICK – Light mark on the surface of a coin, usually from contact with another.

TYPE COIN – Commemoratives of the same design. For example, Alabama and the Alabama 2X2 are the same commemorative type.

APPENDIX B

STATISTICS

Table A-1: RANK OF SILVER & GOLD COMMEMS BY MINTAGE

RANK	ISSUE	MINTAGE
1	'35/4-D Boone	2,003
2	'35/4-S Boone	2,004
3	1938-P Boone	2,100
	1938-D Boone	2,100
	1938-S Boone	2,100
6	1939-P Ark.	2,104
	1939-D Ark.	2,104
8	1939-S Ark.	2,105
9	1937-D Boone	2,506
	1937-S Boone	2,506
11	'39-P Oregon	3,004
	'39-D Oregon	3,004
13	'39-S Oregon	3,005
14	1938-D Ark.	3,155
15	1938-P Ark.	3,156
	1938-S Ark.	3,156
17	1938-D Texas	3,775
18	1938-P Texas	3,780
19	1938-S Texas	3,814
20	Grant/Star	4,256
21	Miss. 2X4	5,000
22	1935-D Boone	5,005
	1935-S Boone	5,005
	1936-D Boone	5,005
	1936-P Cinci	5,005
	1936-D Cinci	5,005
27	1936-S Boone	5,006
	1936-S Cinci	5,006
	'36-S Oregon	5,006
30	'33-D Oregon	5,008
31	1935-D Ark.	5,505
	1937-P Ark.	5,505
	1937-D Ark.	5,505
34	1935-S Ark.	5,506
	1937-S Ark.	5,506
36	'49-P BTW	6,004
	'49-D BTW	6,004
	'49-S BTW	6,004
	'50-P BTW	6,004
	'50-D BTW	6,004
41	'38-D Oregon	6,005
	Ala. 2X2	6,006
	'38-P Oregon	6,006
	'38-S Oregon	6,006
45	'28 Oregon	6,028
46	1937-P Texas	6,571
47	1937-D Texas	6,605
48	1937-S Texas	6,637
49	'51-D BTW	7,004
	'51-S BTW	7,004
51	'34-D Oregon	7,006
52	'53-P W/C	8,003
	'53-D W/C	8,003
54	'48-P BTW	8,005

RANK	ISSUE	MINTAGE
54	'48-D BTW	8,005
	'48-S BTW	8,005
57	'52-D W/C	8,006
	'52-S W/C	8,006
59	1936-S Col.	8,007
60	1936-D Col.	8,009
61	1936-P Texas	8,911
62	1936-P Col.	9,007
63	1936-D Texas	9,039
64	1936-S Texas	9,055
65	1936-P Ark.	9,660
	1936-D Ark.	9,660
67	1936-S Ark.	9,662
68	1937-P Boone	9,810
69	Hawaiian	9,958
70	1935-P Texas	9,996
71	'51-D W/C	10,004
	'51-S W/C	10,004
73	'36 Oregon	10,006
74	1934-P Boone	10,007
	1935-D Texas	10,007
76	'35/4-P Boone	10,008
77	Hudson	10,008
	Sp. Trail	10,008
79	1935-S Texas	10,008
80	1935-P Boone	10,010
81	'54-P W/C	12,006
	'54-D W/C	12,006
83	'37-D Oregon	12,008
84	1936-P Boone	12,012
	1935-P Ark.	13,012
86	Vancouver	14,994
87	'36-D Rh. Island	15,010
88	'36-S Rh. Island	15,011
89	New Rochelle	15,266
90	Missouri	15,428
91	Norfolk	16,936
92	Albany	17,671
93	Antietam	18,028
94	Lynchburg	20,013
	'36-P Rh. Island	20,013
96	Elgin	20,015
97	1921 Pilgrim	20,053
98	Delaware	20,993
99	Isabella	24,214
100	Bridgeport	25,015
	Maryland	25,015
	Wisconsin	25,015
	York	25,015
104	Conn.	25,018
105	Robinson	25,265
106	Gettys.	26,928
107	Pan-Pac	27,134
108	Vermont	28,142

RANK	ISSUE	MINTAGE
109	Roanoke	29,030
110	'36-D San Diego	30,092
111	Lafayette	36,026
112	'26 Oregon	47,955
113	Maine	50,028
114	Cleveland	50,030
115	Alabama	59,038
116	1934-P Texas	61,463
117	Grant	67,405
118	'35-S San Diego	70,132
119	Bay Bridge	71,424
120	Long Is.	81,826
121	'26-S Oregon	83,055
122	Calif.	86,594
123	'47-P BTW	100,017
	'47-D BTW	100,017
	'47-S BTW	100,017
126	Lexington	100,057
127	Iowa	100,058
128	'53-S W/C	108,020
129	'51-P W/C	110,018
130	'54-S W/C	122,024
131	Sesqui	141,120
132	Huguenot	142,080
133	1920 Pilgrim	152,112
134	Lincoln	162,013
135	'46-D BTW	200,113
136	Monroe	274,077
137	'46-S BTW	500,279
138	'51-P BTW	510,082
139	'50-S BTW	512,091
140	1892 Columbian	950,000
141	'46-P BTW	1,000,546
142	Stone Mtn.	1,314,709
143	1893 Columbian	1,550,405
144	'52-P W/C	2,006,292

GOLD COMMEM RANKINGS

RANK	ISSUE	MINTAGE
1	$50 PP Round	483
2	$50 PP Octag.	645
3	1922 Grant	5,000
4	Grant/Star	5,016
5	$2.50 Pan-Pac	6,749
6	1916 McKinley	9,977
7	1917 McKinley	10,000
8	1904 L&C	10,025
9	1905 L&C	10,041
10	$1 Pan-Pac	15,000
11	1903 Jefferson	17,500
12	1903 McKinley	17,500
13	1926 Sesqui	46,019

Harry Laibstain

Table A-2: PCGS & NGC POPULATIONS IN MS64-67 (DEC. 1994 DATA)

ISSUE	MS64 PCGS	MS64 NGC	MS65 PCGS	MS65 NGC	MS66 PCGS	MS66 NGC	MS67 PCGS	MS67 NGC	ISSUE	MS64 PCGS	MS64 NGC	MS65 PCGS	MS65 NGC	MS66 PCGS	MS66 NGC	MS67 PCGS	MS67 NGC
Isabella	505	400	169	175	66	50	12	11	'38-S Oregon	319	91	498	201	230	170	43	29
Lafayette	223	230	75	76	12	13	3	3	'39-P Oregon	179	56	259	127	123	92	22	25
Alabama	386	346	109	77	7	4	0	1	'39-D Oregon	155	42	248	108	167	110	54	53
Ala. 2X2	387	276	111	94	9	5	3	0	'39-S Oregon	170	47	238	117	121	105	30	22
Albany	1,178	396	885	531	274	188	34	22	Pan-Pac	374	365	178	198	67	72	19	15
Antietam	811	260	1,002	438	434	177	84	45	1920 Pilgrim	912	888	353	395	76	44	7	1
1935-P Ark.	445	210	230	136	18	16	3	0	1921 Pilgrim	602	374	278	217	54	12	3	1
1935-D Ark.	315	122	223	117	49	26	5	2	36-P Rh. Isl.	844	381	606	358	170	57	4	3
1935-S Ark.	323	139	227	113	40	24	2	2	36-D Rh. Isl.	705	270	505	271	162	47	5	3
1936-P Ark.	326	167	125	81	26	9	0	2	36-S Rh. Isl.	643	244	359	210	70	25	1	1
1936-D Ark.	403	173	183	132	35	15	5	3	Roanoke	1,174	388	1,360	703	453	312	103	88
1936-S Ark.	381	154	157	146	35	22	2	2	Robinson	1,137	393	479	303	139	68	18	6
1937-P Ark.	265	129	108	66	15	11	0	0	35S San Diego	2,311	576	4,102	1,607	724	139	26	14
1937-D Ark.	283	138	154	99	18	20	3	1	36D San Diego	1,595	455	3,104	843	292	79	12	6
1937-S Ark.	253	119	72	49	7	7	0	1	Sesqui	517	486	66	61	5	1	0	0
1938-P Ark.	175	74	79	47	9	10	1	0	Sp. Trail	673	196	705	265	195	106	25	2
1938-D Ark.	172	85	94	59	17	14	5	3	Stone Mtn.	2,286	947	929	711	229	146	54	23
1938-S Ark.	170	72	66	48	7	3	0	1	1934-P Texas	1,017	313	673	309	97	86	11	11
1939-P Ark.	127	83	53	37	2	4	1	0	1935-P Texas	319	67	566	256	390	214	79	43
1939-D Ark.	136	72	73	55	12	8	1	1	1935-D Texas	314	85	650	252	313	229	47	30
1939-S Ark.	122	74	93	69	15	4	0	1	1935-S Texas	381	92	545	262	125	158	11	13
Bay Bridge	1,122	416	894	496	306	156	43	21	1936-P Texas	374	108	617	259	290	129	31	18
1934-P Boone	332	125	346	188	70	62	10	6	1936-D Texas	271	87	609	252	476	233	90	36
1935-P Boone	385	171	328	189	65	49	8	7	1936-S Texas	400	91	593	256	151	127	11	12
1935-D Boone	291	95	166	80	43	49	2	3	1937-P Texas	309	95	445	193	132	111	20	17
1935-S Boone	209	87	259	178	98	88	7	9	1937-D Texas	282	65	522	243	199	144	22	13
'35/4-P Boone	444	158	382	202	85	81	5	4	1937-S Texas	270	80	463	235	180	151	12	17
'35/4-D Boone	108	49	133	60	61	36	11	8	1938-P Texas	257	57	241	133	64	64	4	12
'35/4-S Boone	138	56	119	72	30	24	1	2	1938-D Texas	185	43	325	131	107	85	14	20
1936-P Boone	508	180	452	243	118	84	7	16	1938-S Texas	211	49	293	121	120	98	11	19
1936-D Boone	328	92	327	155	70	56	5	5	Vancouver	590	368	306	259	62	82	11	9
1936-S Boone	242	83	296	162	93	103	14	9	Vermont	776	507	348	301	86	58	6	4
1937-P Boone	434	164	467	215	123	73	18	10	'46-P BTW	790	216	663	291	100	116	1	13
1937-D Boone	153	66	171	76	57	37	15	10	'46-D BTW	473	140	398	167	57	66	1	10
1937-S Boone	128	43	138	84	40	47	4	10	'46-S BTW	821	140	696	219	104	97	9	14
1938-P Boone	143	68	167	65	39	18	3	5	'47-P BTW	278	43	254	45	8	2	0	1
1938-D Boone	143	56	164	62	57	38	9	12	'47-D BTW	199	26	166	25	7	5	0	1
1938-S Boone	138	52	119	59	39	30	12	13	'47-S BTW	201	45	314	77	20	9	0	0
Bridgeport	1,356	520	839	412	189	61	11	3	'48-P BTW	275	55	366	53	14	6	0	0
Calif.	674	548	320	368	109	179	17	38	'48-D BTW	288	35	359	63	28	13	0	0
1936-P Cinci	366	162	177	84	17	11	1	0	'48-S BTW	230	25	401	117	32	35	0	1
1936-D Cinci	428	172	282	231	75	59	8	4	'49-P BTW	273	50	378	83	34	22	1	0
1936-S Cinci	360	229	82	66	11	3	0	0	'49-D BTW	292	54	375	78	27	19	0	0
Cleveland	1,954	704	887	572	167	113	8	9	'49-S BTW	174	47	505	97	67	30	0	1
1936-P Col.	454	138	516	293	176	164	22	17	'50-P BTW	203	38	301	50	19	4	0	0
1936-D Col.	306	102	481	206	277	268	62	76	'50-D BTW	233	45	280	47	10	7	0	0
1936-S Col.	388	93	449	278	224	270	28	36	'50-S BTW	299	57	579	131	63	46	2	1
'92 Columbian	920	846	300	320	51	47	4	3	'51-P BTW	499	92	257	75	26	6	1	1
'93 Columbian	787	829	183	236	21	27	1	0	'51-D BTW	212	38	279	66	24	18	0	1
Conn.	955	513	520	544	147	108	12	9	'51-S BTW	108	22	418	83	66	43	1	0
Delaware	1,022	449	745	418	207	111	17	12	'51-P W/C	263	73	52	54	3	12	0	1
Elgin	1,424	419	1,217	586	304	185	28	23	'51-D W/C	340	54	166	31	3	5	0	0
Gettys.	1,232	456	676	474	176	74	24	13	'51-S W/C	255	49	422	85	12	27	0	1
Grant	654	597	298	261	58	52	10	6	'52-P W/C	1,189	325	479	350	33	63	0	1
Grant/Star	141	184	40	60	2	13	0	1	'52-D W/C	317	47	102	62	0	1	0	0
Hawaiian	410	261	143	101	16	13	0	0	'52-S W/C	346	49	301	82	14	20	1	0
Hudson	618	340	262	189	48	33	2	1	'53-P W/C	333	38	100	43	2	5	0	0
Huguenot	944	653	427	336	106	49	70	2	'53-D W/C	342	43	80	19	0	1	0	0
Iowa	1,516	352	2,482	962	1,252	683	222	87	'53-S W/C	465	90	287	106	8	25	0	1
Lexington	926	737	299	215	39	21	0	1	'54-P W/C	430	61	136	39	4	12	0	0
Lincoln	1,143	645	489	335	114	62	25	10	'54-D W/C	375	69	93	37	0	4	0	0
Long Is.	1,240	703	481	430	91	78	25	12	'54-S W/C	495	88	282	95	6	22	0	0
Lynchburg	911	344	729	436	232	161	29	31	Wisconsin	941	336	1,540	670	622	415	115	58
Maine	732	474	450	313	137	81	5	5	York	866	234	1,380	554	772	463	273	92
Maryland	1,269	638	636	487	144	91	4	10									
Missouri	290	363	63	62	8	2	0	0	**GOLD COMMEMS**								
Miss. 2X4	258	305	69	58	4	1	0	0									
Monroe	481	538	96	109	27	14	3	3	1903 Jefferson	465	241	285	204	95	71	13	6
New Rochelle	968	272	917	464	297	113	41	15	1903 McKinley	387	179	224	138	98	54	15	3
Norfolk	444	101	896	376	1,005	479	393	99	1904 L&C	237	132	105	58	32	23	4	5
'26 Oregon	778	306	433	187	85	58	8	6	1905 L&C	168	85	62	31	9	3	0	0
'26-S Oregon	891	339	529	380	113	189	30	34	$1 Pan-Pac	674	338	363	212	116	34	7	1
'28 Oregon	371	115	382	184	147	46	18	6	$2.50 Pan-Pac	386	192	251	197	56	45	4	8
'33-D Oregon	452	131	447	162	112	34	17	1	$50 PP Round	19	39	0	9	0	3	0	0
'34-D Oregon	711	256	476	186	91	24	5	1	$50 PP Octag.	10	30	2	6	0	0	0	0
'36 Oregon	517	142	551	279	197	152	37	35	1916 McKinley	599	261	307	95	105	26	5	1
'36-S Oregon	227	67	344	174	194	187	33	61	1917 McKinley	387	150	187	50	66	16	5	0
'37-D Oregon	295	92	734	290	613	350	202	133	Grant	342	124	224	100	84	49	17	2
'38-P Oregon	386	93	477	210	175	96	18	31	Grant/Star	410	152	324	154	159	43	36	6
'38-D Oregon	239	72	515	176	348	213	58	87	Sesqui	1,030	503	164	44	8	1	0	0

Table A-3: RANK OF SILVER & GOLD COMMEMS BY <u>TOTAL MINT STATE</u> CERTIFIED POPULATION (PCGS & NGC COMBINED)

RANK	ISSUE	POPULATION	RANK	ISSUE	POPULATION	RANK	ISSUE	POPULATION
1	'47-D BTW	431	54	1936-P Cinci	1,048	107	'36-P Rh. Island	2,792
2	1939-P Ark.	462	55	1936-S Boone	1,102	108	Maine	2,820
3	1939-D Ark.	482	56	'54-S W/C	1,125	109	Monroe	2,893
4	1939-S Ark.	484	57	1936-S Ark.	1,137	110	1934-P Texas	2,911
5	'35/4-S Boone	515	58	1936-D Boone	1,140	111	'26-S Oregon	2,999
6	1938-S Ark.	518	59	'50-S BTW	1,141	112	Isabella	3,115
7	1938-S Boone	523	60	1936-D Ark.	1,218	113	Vermont	3,155
8	'53-D W/C	527	61	Miss. 2X4	1,244	114	Sesqui	3,167
9	1938-P Ark.	534	62	1934-P Boone	1,262	115	New Rochelle	3,233
10	'35/4-D Boone	535	63	'28 Oregon	1,351	116	Grant	3,237
	1938-P Boone	535	64	'36-S Oregon	1,371	117	Lynchburg	3,324
12	1937-S Boone	547	65	'46-D BTW	1,371	118	Huguenot	3,352
13	'51-P W/C	549	66	1937-P Texas	1,391	119	Robinson	3,420
14	1938-D Ark.	563	67	1935-P Ark.	1,392	120	Delaware	3,457
15	'52-D W/C	565	68	1936-D Cinci	1,400	121	Antietam	3,467
16	1938-D Boone	570	69	'33-D Oregon	1,409	122	Lexington	3,570
17	'53-P W/C	587	70	Ala. 2X2	1,424	123	Conn.	3,613
18	'50-P BTW	588	71	1935-P Boone	1,452	124	Calif.	3,614
19	'50-D BTW	605	72	1937-S Texas	1,457	125	Gettys.	3,767
20	'47-P BTW	607	73	Missouri	1,482	126	Norfolk	3,839
21	'51-D BTW	615	74	'35/4-P Boone	1,529	127	Bridgeport	3,937
22	1937-D Boone	627	75	1937-D Texas	1,531	128	Albany	3,975
23	'51-D W/C	631	76	'38-P Oregon	1,534	129	Maryland	4,013
24	'47-S BTW	658	77	Alabama	1,537	130	Bay Bridge	4,153
	'54-D W/C	658	78	Lafayette	1,549	131	1920 Pilgrim	4,220
26	'51-S BTW	697	79	Hawaiian	1,592	132	Lincoln	4,243
27	1937-S Ark.	715	80	'38-S Oregon	1,628	133	Elgin	4,603
28	'48-P BTW	737	81	1937-P Boone	1,669	134	Long Is.	4,695
29	'54-P W/C	747	82	1935-S Texas	1,686	135	Roanoke	4,860
30	'48-D BTW	757	83	1936-S Texas	1,698	136	Wisconsin	4,863
31	'52-S W/C	802	84	'38-D Oregon	1,732	137	York	4,927
32	'49-P BTW	809	85	1936-P Boone	1,823	138	1893 Columbian	5,401
33	'48-S BTW	815	86	1936-D Col.	1,845	139	1892 Columbian	5,678
34	'51-S W/C	827	87	1936-S Col.	1,856	140	Cleveland	5,961
35	1937-P Ark.	835	88	1936-P Col.	1,873	141	'36-D San Diego	6,556
	'49-D BTW	835	89	1936-P Texas	1,877	142	Stone Mtn.	7,544
37	1935-D Boone	851	90	'36-S Rh. Island	1,908	143	Iowa	7,849
38	'49-S BTW	873	91	'34-D Oregon	1,930	144	'35-S San Diego	10,099
39	1937-D Ark.	885	92	1935-D Texas	1,950			
40	'39-S Oregon	887	93	1935-P Texas	1,975	**GOLD COMMEM RANKINGS**		
41	'39-P Oregon	903	94	1921 Pilgrim	2,002	1	$50 PP Round	198
42	Grant/Star	907	95	'36 Oregon	2,010	2	$50 PP Octag.	253
43	1938-P Texas	929	96	1936-D Texas	2,074	3	1905 L&C	922
44	'39-D Oregon	945	97	'46-S BTW	2,181	4	1904 L&C	1,129
45	1938-S Texas	956	98	Pan-Pac	2,223	5	Grant	1,283
46	1938-D Texas	958	99	'36-D Rh. Island	2,244	6	1917 McKinley	1,501
47	'51-P BTW	999	100	'26 Oregon	2,258	7	Grant/Star	1,519
48	'53-S W/C	1,004	101	Hudson	2,278	8	$2.50 Pan-Pac	1,544
49	1935-D Ark.	1,005	102	'46-P BTW	2,336	9	1903 McKinley	1,829
50	1935-S Boone	1,015	103	Sp. Trail	2,353	10	1903 Jefferson	1,970
51	1936-P Ark.	1,031	104	Vancouver	2,370	11	1916 McKinley	2,500
52	1936-S Cinci	1,037	105	'52-P W/C	2,743	12	$1 Pan-Pac	2,968
53	1935-S Ark.	1,045	106	'37-D Oregon	2,790	13	Sesqui	4,740

Table A-4: RANK OF SILVER & GOLD COMMEMS BY % OF MINTAGE WHICH IS CERTIFIED

RANK	ISSUE	% CERTIFIED
1	'52-P W/C	<1%
	'46-P BTW	<1%
	'50-S BTW	<1%
	'51-P BTW	<1%
	1893 Columbian	<1%
	'46-S BTW	<1%
	'47-D BTW	<1%
	'51-P W/C	<1%
9	1892 Columbian	1%
	Stone Mtn.	1%
	'47-P BTW	1%
	'46-D BTW	1%
	'47-S BTW	1%
	'53-S W/C	1%
	'54-S W/C	1%
	Monroe	1%
17	Sesqui	2%
	Huguenot	2%
19	Alabama	3%
	Lincoln	3%
	1920 Pilgrim	3%
22	Lexington	4%
	'26-S Oregon	4%
	Calif.	4%
25	'26 Oregon	5%
	1934-P Texas	5%
	Grant	5%
28	'54-D W/C	6%
	Maine	6%
	Long Is.	6%
	Bay Bridge	6%
	Lafayette	6%
	'54-P W/C	6%
	'51-D W/C	6%
35	'53-D W/C	7%
	'52-D W/C	7%
	'53-P W/C	7%
38	Iowa	8%
	Pan-Pac	8%
	'51-S W/C	8%
41	'51-D BTW	9%
	'48-P BTW	9%
43	'48-D BTW	10%
	Missouri	10%
	'50-P BTW	10%
	1921 Pilgrim	10%
	'51-S BTW	10%
	'52-S W/C	10%
	'50-D BTW	10%
	'48-S BTW	10%
51	1935-P Ark.	11%
	1936-P Ark.	11%
	Vermont	11%
54	1936-S Ark.	12%
	Cleveland	12%
56	1936-D Ark.	13%
	1934-P Boone	13%
	'36-S Rh. Island	13%
	Isabella	13%
	1937-S Ark.	13%
61	Robinson	14%
	'49-P BTW	14%
	'49-D BTW	14%
	Gettys.	14%
	'36-P Rh. Island	14%
	Conn.	14%
	'35-S San Diego	14%
	1935-P Boone	14%
	'49-S BTW	14%
70	'36-D Rh. Island	15%
	1937-P Ark.	15%
	1936-P Boone	15%
	'35/4-P Boone	15%
74	Bridgeport	16%
	Vancouver	16%
	Hawaiian	16%
	Maryland	16%
	1937-D Ark.	16%
	1938-S Ark.	16%
	Delaware	16%
81	Lynchburg	17%
	Roanoke	17%
	1935-S Texas	17%
	1938-P Ark.	17%
	1935-D Boone	17%
	1937-P Boone	17%
87	1938-D Ark.	18%
	1935-D Ark.	18%
89	1936-S Texas	19%
	1935-S Ark.	19%
	Antietam	19%
	Wisconsin	19%
93	1935-D Texas	20%
	York	20%
	1935-P Texas	20%
	'36 Oregon	20%
	1935-S Boone	20%
98	1936-S Cinci	21%
	1936-P Col.	21%
	1936-P Cinci	21%
	1936-P Texas	21%
	New Rochelle	21%
	1937-P Texas	21%
	Grant/Star	21%
105	1937-S Boone	22%
	'36-D San Diego	22%
	1939-P Ark.	22%
	1936-S Boone	22%
	1937-S Texas	22%
	'28 Oregon	22%
	Albany	22%
112	Norfolk	23%
	1936-D Boone	23%
	Hudson	23%
	1939-D Ark.	23%
	1936-D Texas	23%
	1939-S Ark.	23%
	1936-D Col.	23%
	Elgin	23%
	1936-S Col.	23%
	'37-D Oregon	23%
	1937-D Texas	23%
123	Sp. Trail	24%
	Ala. 2X2	24%
125	1938-P Texas	25%
	1938-S Boone	25%
	Miss. 2X4	25%
	1937-D Boone	25%
	1938-S Texas	25%
	1938-D Texas	25%
131	1938-P Boone	26%
	'38-P Oregon	26%
	'35/4-S Boone	26%
134	'35/4-D Boone	27%
	1938-D Boone	27%
	'38-S Oregon	27%
	'36-S Oregon	27%
138	'34-D Oregon	28%
	1936-D Cinci	28%
	'33-D Oregon	28%
141	'38-D Oregon	29%
142	'39-S Oregon	30%
	'39-P Oregon	30%
144	'39-D Oregon	31%

GOLD COMMEM RANKINGS

1	1905 L&C	9%
2	1903 McKinley	10%
	Sesqui	10%
4	1903 Jefferson	11%
	1904 L&C	11%
6	1917 McKinley	15%
7	$1 Pan-Pac	20%
8	$2.50 Pan-Pac	23%
9	1916 McKinley	25%
10	Grant	26%
11	Grant/Star	30%
12	$50 PP Octag.	39%
13	$50 PP Round	41%

Table A-5: SILVER & GOLD COMMEMS RANKED BY MS64 POPULATION

RANK	ISSUE	MS64 POP	RANK	ISSUE	MS64 POP	RANK	ISSUE	MS64 POP
1	'51-S BTW	126	55	1935-D Texas	395	109	Antietam	1,035
2	'35/4-D Boone	161	56	1937-D Ark.	399	110	'26 Oregon	1,040
3	1937-S Boone	167		'38-S Oregon	399	111	York	1,084
4	1938-S Boone	179	58	1936-D Col.	402	112	Maine	1,124
5	'39-D Oregon	180	59	1936-D Boone	414	113	Calif.	1,162
6	1939-S Ark.	187	60	Lafayette	415	114	'26-S Oregon	1,173
7	'35/4-S Boone	189	61	1935-D Ark.	423	115	Grant	1,180
8	1938-D Boone	193	62	1934-P Boone	432	116	New Rochelle	1,192
9	1939-D Ark.	201	63	1935-S Ark.	433	117	'36-P Rh. Island	1,197
10	1939-P Ark.	204	64	'54-D W/C	443	118	Vermont	1,222
11	1938-P Boone	207	65	'38-P Oregon	446	119	Wisconsin	1,232
12	1937-D Boone	211	66	1936-S Col.	458	120	Lynchburg	1,241
13	'39-S Oregon	213		1936-P Texas	458	121	1934-P Texas	1,298
14	1938-D Texas	216	68	1935-S Texas	462	122	Delaware	1,402
	'49-S BTW	216	69	'28 Oregon	469	123	Conn.	1,427
16	'47-D BTW	218	70	1936-P Ark.	472	124	Robinson	1,461
17	1938-S Ark.	224	71	1936-S Texas	478	125	Bay Bridge	1,471
	'39-P Oregon	224	72	'54-P W/C	483	126	'52-P W/C	1,492
19	1938-D Ark.	229	73	1936-S Ark.	501	127	1893 Columbian	1,522
20	'50-P BTW	232	74	1936-P Cinci	506	128	Roanoke	1,523
21	1938-P Ark.	237	75	Miss. 2X4	525	129	Albany	1,533
22	'47-S BTW	238	76	Norfolk	526	130	Lexington	1,540
23	'51-D BTW	241	77	'53-S W/C	540	131	Huguenot	1,545
24	1938-S Texas	249	78	1935-P Boone	542	132	Gettys.	1,633
25	'48-S BTW	250	79	1936-D Ark.	546	133	Lincoln	1,698
26	'50-D BTW	270	80	1936-S Cinci	555	134	1920 Pilgrim	1,712
27	'36-S Oregon	277	81	'33-D Oregon	558	135	1892 Columbian	1,761
28	1935-S Boone	283	82	'51-P BTW	572	136	Bridgeport	1,794
29	'38-D Oregon	289	83	'54-S W/C	573	137	Elgin	1,806
30	1938-P Texas	294	84	1936-P Col.	577	138	Iowa	1,836
31	Grant/Star	296	85	1936-D Cinci	578	139	Long Is.	1,855
32	'51-S W/C	301	86	'35/4-P Boone	579	140	Maryland	1,882
33	'47-P BTW	312	87	1937-P Boone	580	141	'36-D San Diego	2,035
	'49-P BTW	312	88	Ala. 2X2	584	142	Cleveland	2,574
35	'48-D BTW	315	89	'46-D BTW	594	143	'35-S San Diego	2,853
36	1936-S Boone	320	90	Missouri	614	144	Stone Mtn.	3,118
37	'51-P W/C	329	91	Hawaiian	623			
38	'48-P BTW	331	92	'36 Oregon	639			
39	1936-D Texas	336	93	1935-P Ark.	644			
40	1937-S Texas	341	94	1936-D Boone	658			
41	'49-D BTW	341	95	Alabama	694			
42	1937-D Texas	342	96	Pan-Pac	717			
43	'50-S BTW	343	97	Sp. Trail	831			
44	1937-S Ark.	353	98	'36-S Rh. Island	859			
45	'52-D W/C	360	99	Isabella	889			
46	'53-P W/C	361	100	Vancouver	907			
47	1935-D Boone	370	101	1921 Pilgrim	927			
48	'53-D W/C	371	102	Hudson	932			
49	1935-P Texas	372	103	'46-S BTW	940			
50	'51-D W/C	375	104	'36-D Rh. Island	944			
51	1937-P Ark.	382	105	'34-D Oregon	945			
	'52-S W/C	382	106	Sesqui	962			
53	'37-D Oregon	384	107	'46-P BTW	990			
54	1937-P Texas	393	108	Monroe	999			

GOLD COMMEM RANKINGS

RANK	ISSUE	MS64 POP
1	$50 PP Octag.	35
2	$50 PP Round	54
3	1905 L&C	229
4	1904 L&C	339
5	Grant	438
6	1917 McKinley	508
7	1903 McKinley	529
8	Grant/Star	541
9	$2.50 Pan-Pac	56
10	1903 Jefferson	
11	1916 McKinley	
12	$1 Pan-Pac	
13	Sesqui	

Harry Laibstain

Table A-6: SILVER & GOLD COMMEMS RANKED BY MS65 POPULATION

RANK	ISSUE	MS65 POP	RANK	ISSUE	MS65 POP	RANK	ISSUE	MS65 POP
1	1939-P Ark.	84	55	'47-S BTW	364	109	1936-P Col.	777
2	'53-D W/C	87	56	'39-P Oregon	365	110	'52-P W/C	799
3	Grant/Star	90	57	'53-S W/C	369	111	'36 Oregon	800
4	'51-P W/C	97	58	'48-P BTW	379	112	1935-P Texas	804
5	Miss. 2X4	100	59	'48-D BTW	385	113	1936-S Texas	812
6	1937-S Ark.	106	60	1938-S Texas	390	114	1936-D Texas	834
7	1938-S Ark.	108	61	1893 Columbian	396	115	1936-P Texas	847
	'54-D W/C	108	62	1935-S Boone	417	116	1935-D Texas	868
9	1938-P Ark.	116	63	'49-D BTW	424	117	'46-S BTW	875
10	1939-D Ark.	119	64	'49-P BTW	430	118	Long Is.	878
11	Sesqui	121	65	Hudson	434	119	'26-S Oregon	883
12	Missouri	127	66	1936-S Boone	435	120	'36-P Rh. Island	924
13	'53-P W/C	129	67	1938-D Texas	437		'46-P BTW	924
14	1936-S Cinci	138	68	1921 Pilgrim	451	122	Sp. Trail	940
15	'52-D W/C	139	69	'51-S W/C	467	123	1934-P Texas	941
16	1938-D Ark.	143	70	1936-D Boone	471	124	'37-D Oregon	995
17	1939-S Ark.	145	71	1936-D Cinci	473	125	Conn.	1,007
18	Alabama	149	72	Lexington	477	126	Maryland	1,066
19	Lafayette	152	73	'51-S BTW	480	127	Delaware	1,072
20	'54-P W/C	158	74	'48-S BTW	491	128	Gettys.	1,077
21	1937-P Ark.	160	75	'36-S Oregon	496	129	Lynchburg	1,104
22	'51-D W/C	164	76	1935-P Boone	503	130	Bridgeport	1,169
23	1938-S Boone	169	77	1934-P Boone	506	131	Norfolk	1,237
24	Ala. 2X2	176	78	'36-S Rh. Island	527	132	Bay Bridge	1,314
	'47-D BTW	176	79	Vancouver	535	133	Albany	1,336
26	'35/4-S Boone	177	80	'28 Oregon	541	134	New Rochelle	1,340
27	'35/4-D Boone	181	81	'46-D BTW	542	135	Cleveland	1,365
28	1936-P Ark.	193	82	Grant	546	136	Antietam	1,387
29	Monroe	196	83	'35/4-P Boone	561	137	Stone Mtn.	1,578
30	Hawaiian	203	84	'49-S BTW	561	138	Elgin	1,734
31	1938-D Boone	204	85	'26 Oregon	584	139	York	1,898
32	1938-P Boone	210		'33-D Oregon	584	140	Roanoke	1,998
33	1937-S Boone	212	87	1892 Columbian	604	141	Wisconsin	2,129
34	1937-D Boone	231	88	1937-P Texas	608	142	Iowa	3,335
35	1937-D Ark.	233	89	Vermont	621	143	'36-D San Diego	3,835
36	1935-D Boone	236	90	'34-D Oregon	624	144	'35-S San Diego	5,614
37	1936-P Cinci	238	91	1937-P Boone	643			
38	'47-P BTW	268	92	'38-P Oregon	649			
39	1936-S Ark.	294	93	Calif.	661			
40	'50-D BTW	296	94	1936-D Col.	668			

GOLD COMMEM RANKINGS

RANK	ISSUE	MS65 POP	RANK	ISSUE	MS65 POP
41	1936-D Ark.	297	95	'38-D Oregon	669
42	'51-P BTW	316	96	'50-S BTW	672
43	1935-D Ark.	319	97	1936-P Boone	676
44	'50-P BTW	322	98	Maine	676
45	'51-D BTW	327	99	'38-S Oregon	677
46	1935-S Ark.	333	100	Huguenot	683
47	Isabella	337	101	1937-S Texas	687
48	'39-D Oregon	342	102	1936-S Col.	696
49	'39-S Oregon	343	103	1920 Pilgrim	696
50	Pan-Pac	350	104	'36-D Rh. Island	726
51	'54-S W/C	356	105	1937-D Texas	740
52	1935-P Ark.	361	106	Robinson	749
53	'52-S W/C	362	107	1935-S Texas	762
54	1938-P Texas	363	108	Lincoln	773

GOLD COMMEM RANKINGS

RANK	ISSUE	MS65 POP
1	$50 PP Octag.	8
2	$50 PP Round	9
3	1905 L&C	74
4	Sesqui	149
5	1904 L&C	152
6	1917 McKinley	212
7	Grant	289
8	1903 McKinley	338
9	1916 McKinley	358
10	$2.50 Pan-Pac	430
11	1903 Jefferson	441
12	Grant/Star	456
13	$1 Pan-Pac	528

Certified Commems

Table A-7: SILVER & GOLD COMMEMS RANKED BY MS66 POPULATION

RANK	ISSUE	MS66 POP	RANK	ISSUE	MS66 POP	RANK	ISSUE	MS66 POP
1	'52-D W/C	1	55	1935-D Ark.	67	109	Cleveland	252
	'53-D W/C	1	56	Hudson	68	110	'39-D Oregon	256
3	Miss. 2X4	3	57	1937-S Boone	72	111	1936-S Texas	262
4	1936-S Cinci	4	58	'49-S BTW	73	112	1935-S Texas	267
	'54-D W/C	4	59	'36-S Rh. Island	77	113	Calif.	269
6	Alabama	5	60	1937-D Boone	79	114	'26-S Oregon	277
	1939-P Ark.	5	61	'51-S BTW	80	115	Sp. Trail	285
	Sesqui	5	62	1892 Columbian	81	116	Delaware	295
9	'51-D W/C	7	63	'35/4-D Boone	87	117	1937-S Texas	297
	'53-P W/C	7		1935-D Boone	87	118	1937-D Texas	316
11	1938-S Ark.	8		'50-S BTW	87	119	1936-P Col.	320
	Missouri	8	66	1938-D Boone	89	120	'36 Oregon	334
13	'47-D BTW	9		Grant	89		'36-D San Diego	334
14	'47-P BTW	10	68	'52-P W/C	95	122	Stone Mtn.	349
15	Ala. 2X2	12	69	'34-D Oregon	106	123	Lynchburg	361
16	1938-P Ark.	13	70	1936-D Boone	109	124	'38-S Oregon	362
17	1937-S Ark.	14	71	1935-P Boone	112	125	New Rochelle	363
	Grant/Star	14		1938-P Texas	112	126	'36-S Oregon	368
	'51-P W/C	14	73	1920 Pilgrim	115	127	1936-P Texas	395
20	1939-S Ark.	15	74	Isabella	116	128	Albany	419
21	'48-P BTW	16	75	1936-D Cinci	120	129	Bay Bridge	420
	'50-D BTW	16	76	'26 Oregon	122	130	Elgin	461
	'54-P W/C	16	77	1934-P Boone	125	131	1936-S Col.	475
24	Lafayette	20	78	'46-D BTW	127	132	1935-D Texas	502
	'50-P BTW	20	79	Vancouver	128	133	1936-D Col.	507
26	1939-D Ark.	21	80	Vermont	129	134	'38-D Oregon	532
27	1937-P Ark.	22	81	Pan-Pac	133	135	Antietam	538
28	1936-P Ark.	23	82	'33-D Oregon	135	136	1935-P Texas	563
29	'47-S BTW	24	83	Huguenot	142	137	1936-D Texas	679
30	Hawaiian	25	84	'35/4-P Boone	153	138	Roanoke	717
	'51-D BTW	25	85	Long Is.	158	139	'35-S San Diego	831
32	1938-D Ark.	27	86	Lincoln	168	140	'37-D Oregon	931
	1936-P Cinci	27	87	1934-P Texas	171	141	Wisconsin	991
	'54-S W/C	27	88	'36-D Rh. Island	172	142	York	1,158
35	'48-D BTW	30	89	1938-D Texas	172	143	Norfolk	1,415
36	1935-P Ark.	31	90	Maine	175	144	Iowa	1,782
	'51-P BTW	31	91	'28 Oregon	175			
38	'53-S W/C	32	92	1935-S Boone	177			
39	1937-D Ark.	33	93	1936-P Boone	184			
	'49-D BTW	33		'46-S BTW	184	**GOLD COMMEM RANKINGS**		
	'52-S W/C	33	95	1936-S Boone	185	1	$50 PP Octag.	0
42	Monroe	38	96	1937-P Boone	186	2	$50 PP Round	3
43	'51-S W/C	38	97	'39-P Oregon	190	3	Sesqui	5
44	1936-D Ark.	39	98	'39-S Oregon	197	4	1905 L&C	6
45	1936-S Ark.	42	99	1938-S Texas	199	5	1904 L&C	44
	1893 Columbian	42		'46-P BTW	199	6	1917 McKinley	66
47	1938-P Boone	43	101	Robinson	200	7	$2.50 Pan-Pac	77
	'49-P BTW	43	102	'36-P Rh. Island	201	8	1916 McKinley	105
49	'35/4-S Boone	50	103	Bridgeport	214	9	Grant	111
	'48-S BTW	50	104	Conn.	222	10	$1 Pan-Pac	112
51	Lexington	54	105	1937-P Texas	223	11	1903 Jefferson	115
52	1921 Pilgrim	55	106	Maryland	224	12	1903 McKinley	129
53	1935-S Ark.	60	107	Gettys.	231	13	Grant/Star	175
	1938-S Boone	60	108	'38-P Oregon	242			

Harry Laibstain

Appendix C

REFERENCES

Bowers, Q. David. <u>Commemorative Coins of the United States</u>, A Complete Encyclopedia. Bowers and Merena Galleries, Inc. 1991

Breen, Walter. <u>Walter Breen's Complete Encyclopedia of U.S. and Colonial Coins</u>, F.C.I. Press Inc. & Doubleday. 1988.

The Certified Coin Dealer Newsletter, June 2, 1989. CDN, Torrance, CA.

Ibid, March 25, 1994.

The Coin Dealer Newsletter, January 9, 1970. CDN, Torrance, CA.

Ibid, January 4, 1980.

Ibid, October 1, 1982.

Ibid, June 2, 1989.

Ibid, March 25, 1994.

Iacova, James S. <u>A Comprehensive Guide to United States Coins</u>, The Ivy Press, Inc., Dallas, TX 1979.

NGC Census Report. March 1994, Numismatic Guarantee Corporation of America, Parsippany, NJ.

Ibid, December 1994.

PCGS Population Report. March 1994, Professional Coin Grading Service, Newport Beach, CA.

Ibid, December 1994.

Swiatek, Anthony & Walter Breen. <u>The Encyclopedia of United States Silver and Gold Commemorative Coins: 1892-1954</u>. Arco Publishing, Inc. 1981

Yeoman, R.S. <u>A Guide Book of United States Coins</u>. 10th Edition, Western Publishing Company, Racine, WI.

Ibid, 23rd Edition.

Ibid, 47th Edition.

ABOUT THE AUTHOR

Harry Laibstain was born in Norfolk, Virginia in 1957 and grew up in Virginia Beach. He majored in Economics and Philosophy at The College of William and Mary, graduating in 1980. Harry was then accepted to the Marshall Wythe Law School and was making preparations to attend. However, during that summer his childhood interest in coins had been rekindled by the 1979-1980 silver boom. He rented a small retail space from an uncle in the jewelry business and by the end of the summer had decided to forgo law school and take a chance on coins. Harry Laibstain Rare Coins was formed the summer of 1980.

In the early '80's, before certification, Harry dealt heavily with collector series and circulated coins. His original interest was in Morgan and Peace dollars. Other specialties included Seated dimes and Seated dollars. As his numismatic tastes became more sophisticated he dealt less with circulated grades and more with mint-state and proof coins. Attracted by the designs and low mintages of commemoratives, his interests grew into a full-blown specialty by 1984.

Having actively traded commemoratives through both certified bull markets, Harry has handled every issue in nearly every grade. He is a major participant on the electronic bidding exchanges, posting thousands of bids for commemoratives. His reputation as a buyer and source for commemoratives is widely known among the numismatic community.